DATE

# The Evans Guide for
# HOUSETRAINING YOUR DOG

# The Evans Guide for
# HOUSETRAINING YOUR DOG

---

## by Job Michael Evans

*With Photographs by*
*Charles P. Hornek*

First Printing—First Edition
1987

HOWELL BOOK HOUSE Inc.
230 Park Avenue
New York, N.Y. 10169

**Library of Congress Cataloging-in-Publication Data**

Evans, Job Michael.
   The Evans guide for housetraining your dog.

   Includes index.
   1. Dogs—Training.  I. Title.  II. Title: Housetraining your
dog.
SF431.E95   1987      636.7'0887      86-21143
ISBN 0-87605-542-0

# Contents

# Acknowledgments

---

I WOULD LIKE to thank the members of the veterinary community who are often the first to hear about a housetraining problem and often refer clients my way: Dr. Lewis Berman, Dr. Sally Haddock, Dr. Gene Solomon, Dr. Stephen Kritsick, Dr. Malcolm Kram, Dr. Stuart Brodsky, Dr. Jane Bicks, Dr. Gerald Johnson, Dr. Howard Kessler, Dr. Adrian Alexandru and others too numerous to mention here.

I would also like to thank fellow trainers Carol Lea Benjamin and Marie Ehrenberg, as well as Jack and Wendy Volhard and Don Arner.

Special thanks to Dr. Myrna Milani and to Dr. Stephanne Hazen.

My thanks also to the staff at the American Kennel Club library, and to the staff at Howell Book House.

Special thanks to Kathryn Clancy and her dog Seamus, as well as to Beverly Higgins, operator of Sunni New York Tanning Parlor, for use of her dog Bunde as well as for my year-round suntan!

The Animal Nutrition Center provided props and Marcia Habib at Sutton Dog Parlor graciously groomed my models. My thanks.

Special thanks go to my photographer, Charles Hornek and my typist, Jody Milano.

Finally, my thanks to each of my private clients who have followed my ACCESS Plan and had SUCCESS in housetraining their pets.

# Introduction

I ORIGINALLY THOUGHT of titling this book *You Dirty Dog!* but that was in a moment of temporary insanity and unreality. The fact is, most dogs desperately *want* to be housetrained. What holds up the process? Usually the fumbles, foibles, misunderstandings and misconceptions of their *human* keepers. But titling the book *You Dirty Owner!* just didn't have that familiar ring to it, and I didn't think it would sell too many copies since dogs don't yet dole out cash. Besides, humans are too sensitive a species to appreciate a title like that.

I don't have any concrete statistics as to the number of dogs who are euthanized because of an inability on the part of the owner (and sometimes the dog) to surmount housetraining problems, but I suspect the number is very high. In fact, in giving seminars to shelter personnel and in private consultations with Ms. Mickey Niego, who works in the education department at New York's ASPCA, I suspect it is the *number one* behavioral reason why dogs are given up on and taken to shelters.

Don't get me wrong—I'm not at all blaming shelter workers. Their job has pleasant and not-so-pleasant aspects and it is not their fault that we have a tremendous surplus of animals in our country. Shelter personnel spend countless hours on the phone trying to explain how to housetrain puppies and dogs, and for this they are to be commended. Perhaps this book will help them even more.

It is my firm belief that the state of dog training and care is today where child care and training were about 100 years ago—before Anna Freud, Dr. Benjamin Spock or any experts began the process of enlightening parents on how to parent. Back then, toilet training was one of the most misunderstood areas of child care and mythology and folklore abounded. Some kids just didn't get toilet trained until they were four or even five (we know the process can be accomplished in less time today) and many a child was screamed at, berated, spanked and even battered when they made "mistakes" after the parents had decided or decreed that accidents were no longer acceptable. To get advice, distraught daughters talked to their mothers, who, of course, handed down the folklore "remedies" they had been given by *their* mothers. Oral tradition is a great teaching tool, but not when it transmits inaccurate information. Today, toilet training for children is still a task, but no mother has to look long or hard for accurate advice.

The above scenario serves as a model for what has been happening in the area of housetraining puppies and dogs. To be sure, the discussions of the process are still glutted with folklore. As recently as 1985 one training book advised owners to "hold his nose to the floor," give the dog a hard slap and put vinegar on the dog's nose. But many good explanations of the housetraining ritual *have* appeared and I have tried to incorporate the best and most progressive methods with my own distinct approach. My caution to you is to watch what you read—you can be a victim of misinformation quite unknowingly.

If you've been reading books about housetraining and have been finding a lot of contradictory advice—I understand your confusion. Don't let it get to you. I've tried to combine the best research and comments here to dispel folklore and clear up confusion.

Please don't view housetraining as an isolated process with one magic solution—if you're looking for that in this book, you're not going to get it. Housetraining is a part of your *overall relationship* with your dog. You have to check your Alpha status, your paralanguage, your nutrition, your schedule and the structure of your environment.

But many owners want desperately to believe that there is a magic solution to the housetraining woes—a "secret method" that can be imparted to the reader (preferably in two minutes) that will make the problem go away overnight. My friends, that's just not the case. It takes more time to understand housetraining than that. The time you save in screaming and yelling at your dog, chasing him or her all over the house, stepping in mistakes and laboriously scrubbing up accidents or replacing ruined carpets might very well add up to eighty times the amount of time it will take to read this book. And besides, the tips you will pick up here for resolving (or preventing) a housetraining problem will also help you to avoid *other* behavioral problems that often crop up along with a housetraining difficulty.

Finally, by way of introduction, I want to extend to new puppy owners my ardent hope that you will never have a housetraining problem, and to those of you who do, my sincere sympathy and, of course, my advice. You see, I've been where you are many times over. While I was at New Skete Monastery, famous for raising and training dogs, I housetrained over 35 puppies who were personal pets, many older dogs, and some of the worse recalcitrants you can imagine—like the five-year-old Labrador Retriever who would defecate on my bed, and then meticulously pull the covers over the gift he had left. Once while attempting to train this particular canine criminal I came back to my bedroom and fell into bed, exhausted from a day of training dogs. Cute, huh?

Then there was the poodle who would vomit and defecate *at the same time*, giving me two messes to clean up for the price of one. Let's not forget the Bichon Frise who managed to "hold it" and not defecate for almost five days (apparently she knew she was being trained and went on strike). She gave *me* emotional diarrhea in the process.

Now that I have my own business in New York, I see many housetraining cases each week. So I've been there and back. I dedicate this book to owners who want to prevent housetraining problems or who want to correct them, and most of all to the dogs I have known who have cleaned up their act.

# 1

# The ACCESS Plan

---

**M**Y METHOD FOR GETTING puppies or older dogs housetrained can be summed up by the word ACCESS. This is a word to keep in mind as you proceed through the housetraining process:

**A** . . . is for *Alpha*—that's you.
**C** . . . is for *Corrections*—that's what you give.
**C** . . . is also for *Confinement*—that's what you provide.
**E** . . . is for *Establish*.
**S** . . . is for a *Schedule* (which is what you *establish!*).
**S** . . . is also for *Selecting* a dog food that will aid you in getting your dog housetrained.

Remember, A-C-C-E-S-S: Become Alpha to your dog, correct the dog if necessary using natural corrections outlined herein, confine your pet until housetraining is complete, establish a schedule that you'll stick to and select a good dog food. Following the ACCESS Plan should provide you with ready access to getting your dog fully housetrained.

# 2

# In the Beginning: The Bitch

DID YOU KNOW THAT someone already took a crack at housetraining your puppy? While I know you wouldn't wish the task on anyone, someone already gave it a try—your pup's mother. The bitch is the first Alpha or leader figure to educate the pup that cleanliness is next to godliness. Let me explain what happens.

When a puppy is first born it can crawl and suck and find its mother's teat. It is very sensitive to warmth or cold but it cannot see or hear. In fact, during the first two or three weeks of its life it cannot even urinate or defecate without oral stimulation from the bitch. The mother dog knows this instinctively, so she stimulates the genital area of each puppy (often as it nurses) and then consumes the urination or defecation. We might think this is gross, but it is actually a very common scenario in many mammals. Cats do it too. The puppy learns that it actually pleases mom to defecate and that mom then cleans it all up. This is why it is bad for your puppy or older dog to see you clean up after the dog has an accident in the wrong place. It can foster regressive behavior in the pup. But more on that later.

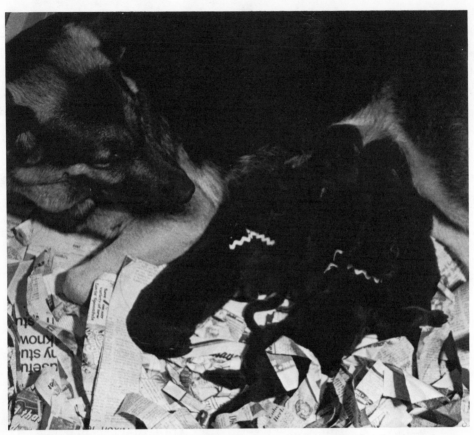

The bitch is the first Alpha or leader figure that educates the puppies that cleanliness is next to godliness.

At about three or four weeks of age there is a transitional period when the pup's eyes and ears open. About this time the pup becomes more aware of its environment. The mother is still cleaning up at this point, but probably the breeder (or whoever is raising the puppies) has started to introduce solid food, usually in the form of some kind of gruel. Depending on the food fed, the stools become more or less noxious, and larger. The bitch stops consuming the stools. The mother starts to inform the pups in no uncertain terms *not* to urinate or defecate near her. She does this by making eye contact and growling at them very softly. Unlike humans, bitches do not scream or bark at their pups to keep order in their litters. Perhaps the dam will discipline by giving the pup a slight shake by the scruff of its neck. Depending on the pup involved and the bitch's perception of it, this slight shake might escalate into an Al Capone shakedown. The point the dam is making is, "Don't do it near me—it smells, and I have a sensitive nose; it's bigger now and more fully formed, and I don't want to lie in it." And finally, "It doesn't taste like it used to for some reason and I'm not consuming it anymore—take it away from me."

Now, *if*—and it's a big *if*—the breeder has provided enough space and a structural set-up that allows the pups to retreat from the mother to eliminate, they will. "Distance the defecation" will become the pup's new rule of thumb. If the pups are enclosed in tight quarters with their mother and have no other recourse, they will *have* to eliminate near her and either she will discipline them or just resign herself to living with her litter in filth. For further advice concerning this period of time and how the structural set-up can influence the owner's chance for successful housetraining, pet store operators and breeders should consult the chapters directed to them later in this book.

It is interesting to note that the time during which a mother dog refuses to consume defecation or urination and packs the pups off to a far corner is precisely the same time that the pups enter a critical period, the period when social relationships are formed and they first learn who is a boss or Alpha figure, and who is a peer or littermate. The pups start to master *paralanguage* about this time, interpreting the low growl of the mother as a reprimand and the whining or yelping of littermates as distress or a signal to play. All of this later influences how the pup views the *owner* when he or she tries to correct or fails to correct a housetraining snafu. Remember, the pup learned its first communicative skills not from you but in its litter, from the bitch and from littermates. It is *this* interaction that will influence the pup for the rest of its life. The words, tonalities and body postures of humans will be forever interpreted and decoded in the light of what was learned during this period. Your dog interprets you on the level of your tonality. While your dog can eventually learn some words in English (like "heel," "stay," "sit," "wanna go out," etc.) he will never be fluent in it. *You*, then, must learn "dogese"—and educate yourself in how your tonality influences your dog.

It is always best to go back as much as possible to this period if you want to prevent or correct housetraining problems or, for that matter, *any* behavior problem. Since few of you will have the opportunity, time or patience to view the interaction of bitches and puppies, I'll teach you some discipline techniques that will simply be variations on what your dog's mother did when the pup had an accident.

If your dog was an orphan pup (perhaps the bitch died giving birth or the puppy and mother were separated) or if your puppy comes from a large litter (over eight pups) you may experience more trouble housetraining your dog. I say you *may* have more trouble, but in the same breath I do not want this to be used as a justification for letting your dog soil at will. But the fact is, the orphan pup misses out on the education the bitch provides concerning cleanliness, and the member of a large litter might "get away" with more mistakes simply because even the *best* mother cannot be everywhere every time to growl at, shake or scold the pup who eliminates in the wrong place.

As a child from an abnormally large family (I have ten brothers and sisters—spaced just a year apart), I know that my mother went dizzy getting us toilet trained (we all are, however). One kid would be having an accident in his or her diapers while mom was coaxing another in the bathroom. It gets hectic, as any canine mother would agree (if they could talk). Like many

18

human moms, some bitches just throw up their paws and say, "What's a mother to do?" They let the pups eliminate just a little closer to them (but rarely *on* them—there are limits) and, in essence, leave the housetraining job, or at least part of it, to the human mother or father who will inherit the puppy. So if you are having a difficult time housetraining your dog, there might be a hook-up here if your dog was an orphan or from a large litter. But again, I stress that this does *not* mean that the puppy can't be housebroken or that you should not select an orphan or a pup with a lot of brothers and sisters.

Then, too, there are various styles of canine mothering, just as there in the human species. Some bitches are born organizers and keep tight control of their brood. They almost dictate the time for defecation and are very strict with even the first infraction of the rules. Other mothers (especially bitches who are having their first litter) don't care as much and will let mistakes slide. At best, even the greatest super-mom will only be able to do a partial job of housetraining, since she simply doesn't have to deal with the intricacies of opening doors, shredding newspapers, teaching a pup to "hold it" or cleaning up messes (at least not after the third week). But her level of competence will affect the task for the human owner, and that is why I stress that it is important to get a puppy from a reputable breeder out of a smart mom. If the canine father is an Einstein, so much the better, but if you are shopping for a puppy from a breeder, try to meet the mom. You should do this, anyway, for a great many reasons, but an informed selection may very well make the housetraining task more smooth.

I can promise you that none of this is conjecture or hearsay, even though this outline of the bitch as "first housetraining expert" may be new information even for experienced breeders. I observed over 300 litters during my years at the New Skete Monastery, and in the process memorized the partial housetraining process that bitches guide their pups through. It is educational that basic housetraining is one of the *first* skills that most bitches attempt to teach their puppies. That means that basic cleanliness can't be all that hard for a pup to master. It's just not the chore or drudgery that humans make it out to be—

otherwise, why would the bitch be so successful at it? In fact, it is when humans come on the scene and *fail* to mimic the bitch that problems result. *In short, when humans humanize housetraining the result is havoc.*

And just why did your pup's mom insist on teaching the puppies cleanliness? Because she didn't want to get eliminated on? Because she didn't like unpleasant odors? Because she didn't want her beautiful coat soiled? Yes, partially. But most of all, she made it a priority because she knew, instinctively, that she had to be *Alpha* over her children, just as her mother was over her. Teaching cleanliness was the first opportunity to establish her authority. As Carol Benjamin says in her brilliant book, *Mother Knows Best* (Howell Book House, 1985):

> With all the assurance, serenity and natural wisdom of her species, a mother dog teaches her young with a dazzling economy of effort. She almost never has to repeat her action a second time in order to be effective. She never loses patience, gets frustrated, gives up. Yet, neither does she harm her puppies with an inappropriate use of force or an unnatural withdrawal of her affection. She knows just what to correct and precisely what to ignore. Her timing is sheer perfection. Her priorities are admirably fitting. Each mother keeps her puppies safe and, in a few short weeks, teaches them much of what they have to know in order that their survival be ensured. It is easily evident that mother knows best. She is a sterling example of teaching and loving at its finest.

Are you Alpha over your dog? You must be. Your dog deserves nothing less. If you aren't, don't expect success in housetraining—in fact, expect countless accidents. How do you get to be Alpha and in essence continue the bitch's role in housetraining? Read on.

# 3

# You as Alpha

---

 $I$ N EVERY WOLF PACK there is a leader, or Alpha figure. This wolf—sometimes a male, sometimes a female—controls many aspects of pack life, including, to a degree, defecation and urination rights and spots. Dogs, of course, are directly descended from wolves and now live in human packs. Problems arise when an individual dog, either through its genetic makeup or mistraining by its owner, comes to think of itself as the leader of the pack.

If your dog thinks that it is Alpha, you are in trouble. How can you know? Usually if you have behavior problems with your dog, you are not considered Alpha no matter how you yourself think you are viewed by the dog. Recently I had a client, a rather bearish woman of imposing build, who informed me during the interview that she knew all about pack theory and that "there is *no way* that my dog doesn't think of me as the Alpha." There was a period on the end of that sentence that indicated absolute finality. I wasn't about to argue the point with her, since my job is basically one of advice and education, but I did think quite another point was made when, during the interview, her terrier came over and squirted urine on her pant suit. Some Alpha!

One way to develop your Alpha role is to get eye contact. Here's an informal example. A more formal method is outlined in the text.

## Eye Contact

One way to develop your Alphahood is to simply get your dog's eye. You might think that your dog looks at you quite frequently, but take a moment to think about the *terms*. They are usually the dog's. Does your dog look at you but only when he or she feels like it? That's not eye contact—that's the dog looking at you because it wants something. You can establish eye contact *on your terms* by formalizing the look-at-me process.

Take your dog, on leash, and sit it. Hold a little upward tension on the lead and bend down and touch your dog's muzzle, and immediately bring your hand up to your eyes. At the same time, make a clicking sound and issue a sentence like, "Tippy, look up here at me right now." Don't just say the dog's name or "Tippy, look." It won't be enough to get the dog to lock eyes with you. That's what you're aiming for—three to four seconds of solid eye contact when the dog looks up at you with an attitude of "your wish is my command." Make sure after you touch your dog's muzzle and then your eyes that you straighten up right away so that the dog truly looks up *at you* and not you down at the dog. Once you have the *lock,* end the moment with some light verbal (not physical) praise such as, "Good boy, Tippy!" Then turn and go about your day. Don't worry about leaving the dog sitting there wondering, "What was *that* all about?" Your dog will soon realize that what it is about is *look at me when I ask you to look, watch me, get out of your own little world, dog, and into mine.* This is a wonderful foundation for any puppy or older dog (especially if housesoiling is a problem) because the eye contact starts to overflow into regular, daily life so that your dog looks at you from across a room. Then *you* can catch your dog's eye more readily to direct it to not do something, like housesoil.

# 4

# Corrections

---

**Y**OUR DOG'S MOTHER used eye contact as one of the first techniques to keep her litter in line. If the initial eye contact wasn't enough to get her desired result she would add a low growl. *Grrrrrrrrrrrrrrrr.* I said low, not loud. In fact, from what I've observed, the growl is barely audible, but the puppy gets the point.

Under what circumstances would the mother find it necessary to discipline her puppies? Well, how about: "You're nursing too long and I want to sleep. Stop it now." "You're playing too roughly with your littermate. Stop it now." "You're circling around as if you are going to eliminate. Take it away from me."

There is one important point to remember: the bitch never negotiated with her puppies. Bitches are singularly untalented at diplomacy. If the undesired behavior is not refrained from immediately, the bitch never starts barking or screeching at her pups (humans do that). She just gets physical, pronto. Don't dialogue with your dog, because the mother never yelled at her puppies. While older dogs might bark (yell) at each other and littermates might converse in whiny tones or bark at or with each other, mother dogs rarely bark at their puppies when disciplining.

So if you've been yelling at your dog when dealing with a housetraining accident resolve to stop today. Try using the human equivalent of the bitch's growl. While making eye contact, speak to your dog in a low, warning tone of voice. Make your voice quite throaty and use a sentence instead of just the dog's name and "no." For many dogs just the dog's name is not enough, nor is just "Bad dog." You must *elongate* the warning phrase to have it more closely resemble the mother's growl, to give the puppy more time to register on the sound, and for general effect. Yet, you must *not* scream, shriek, screech or whine.

If you think back, you might remember times when your own mother used the above technique with you, or when you might have used it with your own children. I'm told that I was hard to toilet train (perhaps that's why I have sympathy for the dog who makes mistakes). When the diapers finally came off (not at age ten, as has been rumored) and I was on my own, my mother attempted to direct me to the bathroom by saying, "Mike, bathroom." This didn't work. But when she lowered her voice and said, "Michael Richard Evans, make it to that bathroom or else," I managed to get there in record time. My mother had, in essence, growled at me.

In fact, a lot of mammals lower their vocal intonation and elongate their warning "phrases" when they are serious. Cats do, and lions and tigers, too. Even moose do. There's a message here for you as a mammal trying to train another mammal. Heed it.

Unfortunately, most owners humanize their discipline instead of following the mother dog's example. Chief among these humanization techniques is using different implements to discipline. I've confiscated from clients over the years quite an array of "weapons": rolled up newspapers, spatulas, hairbrushes, car aerials, ping pong paddles, belts and even a baseball bat.

Besides the fact that these objects are inhumane when used to discipline a dog, they are just not historically valid because the mother dog never ran to get a rolled up newspaper (or a fly swatter or a hairbrush) if her puppy was bad. Don't use *any* implements to discipline your dog!

26

## The Shake

You *should* discipline your dog for unacceptable behavior, such as housetraining accidents, especially if you catch the dog in the act. The most you will need, except in chronic cases, is your growling tone of voice and eye contact. It may, in some cases, be possible to discipline the puppy or older dog for accidents after the fact, but this is a touchy area and will need a chapter of its own (see Chapter 11).

Occasionally, though, especially if the problem is pronounced, it might be necessary to get physical if the dog continues to have accidents even after being disciplined by the growl and eye contact. Many canine mothers, if the puppy fails to respond to eye contact and the growl, will then use the shake: the mother grabs the puppy by the scruff of the neck, shakes it and then may drop or even throw the puppy to the ground. Try adapting this technique with your own dog. Instead of grabbing from above as mom did, reach from underneath with both hands and elevate the dog off its front feet into the air. You should make this switch and reach from underneath instead of grabbing the scruff because when we bring pups into human society we make the top of the head the locus of affection, and we don't want to create a hand-shy dog. The technique is simply an *inversion* of what the mother did and will feel the same to the pup.

## The Swat

Another site for disciplining your dog is under the chin. With closed fingers, swat your dog under the chin, scolding and making eye contact as you do. It is usually easiest to stand with the dog on your left side, so that your right hand can more easily deliver the correction. Be sure to keep some upward pressure on your dog's collar so that you can hold the dog in one place (preferably sitting) as you discipline. Your dog doesn't wear a collar? Terrible!

Put a collar on your dog right away—and if necessary a short one-foot tab leash. You *must*, repeat *must*, have some way of getting your dog immediately if you need to correct it. If you have reached for your dog and it has gotten away from you, even *once*, and scampered about the house teasing you and playing "catch me"—you have been lowered to littermate status and are most definitely *not* seen as an Alpha figure. Bitches pin their puppies, make eye contact with them, shake them and swat them—wham, bam, and the pup says "thank you ma'am." Short and sweet. No negotiations, no dialogue. Littermates chase each other, and enjoy it. Alpha or littermate? Leader or peer? The choice is yours, but you'll have less choice if you can't even *get* the dog to discipline it. So have your dog wear a collar and if necessary a short tab leash (long enough to just touch the floor when the dog is standing) to allow you to even more effectively and quickly get your canine criminal. Just let the dog wear the tab whenever you are home—use a metal tab if he chews it. Even if he looks like a fool strolling around with it on, you'll appreciate the tab because it will give you psychological peace of mind, knowing that you can get your dog if it divebombs under a bed, or gets you going on a wild goose chase. I've found that wearing the tab leash for seven to ten days also serves as a kind of "string-around-the-finger" (or paw, if you prefer) reminder to the dog, a constant indication that the heat is on.

You should remember that dogs are not children, nor are they little people with fur coats on. Parents who would never use *any* degree of physical force with children are free to act on those feelings, but if they interviewed any brood bitch she would inform them that the philosophy does not apply to her species. Dogs are not children. Remember that dogs grow up and mature much more quickly than human infants and their acceptance of verbal and physical discipline is on a different level than that of human children. Don't be afraid to discipline your dog—but discipline humanely and on a level that the dog can comprehend because the discipline mimics that of the bitch.

# 5

# Specific Corrections for Housesoiling

I MUST BEGIN with a caution. In mapping out discipline techniques I fully realize that readers who are overbearing, brutish and overphysical with their dogs might abuse the techniques. I label these owners "Blamers" in my book, *The Evans Guide for Counseling Dog Owners.* The voice is hard and tight, sometimes (but not always) low, even shrill. These owners make up about 30 percent of the dog-owning population, in my opinion. There *is* a risk that if you tell a Blamer *anything* about discipline before, during or after a housesoiling accident, the Blamer may take such information as permission to *over*discipline.

This is a risk I have to take as an author. I took it back in 1978 when I penned the chapter, "Discipline: The Taboo Topic," when I co-wrote *How to Be Your Dog's Best Friend*—then the first book to include a full chapter on exactly what to do if the dog is naughty. I had learned discipline techniques by watching the monastery bitches at work with their litters, and I felt a need to communicate this information in human terms.

If you are the type of person who flies off the handle easily or has an instantly ignited temper, you should check this in yourself. I can almost guarantee that you will not get your dog housebroken if you beat it up or batter it. All that will happen is that the dog will focus on your *correction* rather than the *connection* you want to make. And, believe me, corrections without connections are a dead-end for a dog.

## Paralanguage

Let me tell you about the verbal element in discipline and the phenomenon of what behaviorists call *paralanguage*. Dogs don't speak or use words, but they do have a system of sounds with which they communicate meaning. A puppy learns this paralanguage in the litter setting, which is where the pup learns its first communicative skills. As I mentioned, the Alpha growls, and littermates whine, whimper or yelp. When the dog gets older it expands its paralanguage skills to include howling, rapid barking and so on. But in the beginning, the dividing line in terms of paralanguage between Alpha figures and littermates is pretty clear: use a low tone and you get regarded as Alpha; whine, whimper or yelp and you get demoted to littermate status.

Because most humans don't know anything about the emotional language of the dog we use paralanguage incorrectly in our own speech. We will say, for instance, a sentence in a whiny voice—"Pleeeeze, don't doooo that Tippy"—and the resulting tonality will sound like a littermate whine.

On his recording *Dogtalk*, Dr. Michael Fix gives a rundown of these sounds and when mimicking the whines, whimpers and yelps of puppies he notes that these "are distress, attention-seeking, infantile noises" that littermates make amongst themselves in order to indicate that they are hungry, confused, in distress or even in severe pain. Even if you are saying something that in English (or French or German or any human tongue) is quite serious, for instance, "Tippy, don't you ever mess in my house again," if the tonality—the paralanguage—isn't proper, whatever you say might backfire. If it comes out as, "Tippieeee, don't you *evver* mess in my house againnnnnnn," the message will be decoded as a littermate whine by the puppy.

Unfortunately, it is next to impossible for me to fully explain in a book just how you should and should not sound when reprimanding your dog. But, despite the fact that no recording accompanies this book, I have to give it a try because it is all-important. Besides playing around with phonetic spellings like I did above, let me use two actresses in an analogy. If you sound more like the actress Bea Arthur ("Maude," "Golden Girls") and less like Marilyn Monroe you are bound to have more success when you reprimand your dog for a housetraining accident.

Men should try to sound more like Robert Redford (but *not* John Wayne) and less like Truman Capote. Some women and some men have to make a conscious effort to *lower* their voices an octave when disciplining in order to be effective. A degree in acting isn't necessary, but you should learn how to *act angry,* even when you think some naughty nuisance the dog pulled is just hilarious.

With these cautions firmly in mind, we'll proceed to my prescription for correcting housetraining mistakes. Memorize this list, then rememorize it. While it *may* be possible to discipline your puppy or dog after the fact (see the special chapter on this), for now we'll concentrate on what to do if you catch the dog in the act.

1. First and foremost, if you come upon an accident or catch the puppy or dog in the act *don't scream!* Don't call the puppy to you to discipline it, go toward the dog and don't say anything—unless the puppy is literally squatting and in the middle of eliminating, in which case you may begin gently scolding the puppy as you approach. It is best to sidestep in toward the puppy. Avoid a head-on approach if possible.
2. Reach for the pup's collar and sit the pup in front of the urination or defecation, quickly. Keep some upward tension on the collar, to keep the pup in the sit position. Don't begin disciplining until the pup is sitting. It is no

sense disciplining a puppy or dog that is squirming to get out of your control. Often if you have the puppy wear a training collar (commonly called a "choke chain"), inserting your index finger in one ring and pulling up will give you a sit—if not, push the dog's rump down while simultaneously pulling the ring of the collar up. But don't use a training collar if your pup is not supervised. Use a regular flat collar then.

3. Tilt the dog's head up toward yours for just a second to let it see the displeasure in your eyes. For most breeds you'll probably be stooping down next to the dog, and the right-hand side of the pup is best.

4. Now, after just one to two seconds of eye contact, tilt the pup's head back *down* toward the accident. *Do not put the dog's nose in the mess*—that advice is pure folklore. But do have the pup look at the accident. Often, taking a finger and tracing a line back and forth between the dog's eyes and the urination or defecation will help to make the connection (you do not have to touch the elimination!).

5. Quietly scold the puppy using your elongated sentence, but do *not* whine, scream, shout, use an implement or otherwise get hysterical. Make your scolding just two to three seconds long. *Do not* use physical discipline unless it is indicated in Chapter 11, "Discipline After the Fact," and never for pre-twelve-week-old puppies.

6. Now trot the puppy or older dog by its collar to where it is supposed to relieve itself. Do this as quickly as possible. Here several cautions are necessary, and they may or may not apply depending on where you live:

   a. If you have a backyard, trot the puppy out to it by stooping down and taking the collar and leading the dog out. *Do not pick the dog up to take it to the desired area*. If you do, the dog could interpret that it only has to use that area if you pick it up and put it in the area. That is not the case, for the message is: "*You* take *your* four feet and go to the area prescribed!"

   b. The above is ditto for papers, terraces or the street.

c. If you must take your dog down to the street after an accident (which you must do in order to give a correction with a connection), you must remind the dog of your displeasure on the way without again disciplining the dog on the same level as you did at the scene of the crime. To do this, just give a smart leash tug (diagonally, upward toward yourself) and emit a low growling phrase ("It better not happen again") as you wait for the elevator, or go down the stairs or through the lobby. Otherwise, the dog might be happy-go-lucky by the time it trots through the lobby and will have forgotten what the correction was all about, and certainly won't be open to the *connection* (take it *outside*!). Instead the dog will say, "Wow! I mess and he disciplines me and then I get a walk! Good deal!"

7. Leave your dog out in the yard or out on the street for only two to three minutes. You don't want it cavorting around having a gay old time after the discipline—you just want to make the connection. When I trot the dog to the desired area often I will rap the surface of that area (the papers, concrete or grass, whatever applies) a few times with my index finger saying, "*Here*, this is where you *go*!"—again in a low, firm voice—and then leave.

8. While the dog is in the desired area (hopefully shaking in its boots and repenting its sins and making the right connections), you return and clean up the mess. Try your best not to let the dog see you clean up (more on this later).

9. Retrieve the dog and isolate it for at least thirty minutes, either behind a gate or in a crate. Everything cannot be A-OK after a serious incident. If you cannot physically isolate the dog, at least remain passive for one-half hour. Just go about your business as if you do not have a dog. Don't keep berating the dog but don't coddle it. The dog needs some time to pull itself together. That's in his genetic makeup. There is a

natural reaction of submission after effective discipline and you should cash in on this period, not thwart it, no matter how emotionally strung out *you* are over having to discipline your pet. The dog needs some time to adjust. Let him have it. On the other hand, if your dog is jumping up on you, barking wildly or just acting pushy after a housetraining reprimand, chances are your correction did not get through and wasn't strong enough. Your dog (if post twelve weeks of age) *may* then be a candidate for physical discipline, but consult Chapter 4 for advice on this.

10. After one-half hour, do something nice with the dog, but not overly nice. Play fetch (but make it a short game) or wrestle lightly (no mouthing!) but don't let play predominate. You want to make up after discipline but the general message you want to leave with the dog is that something earth shattering, catastrophic and very bad has happened and it better not happen again.

Finally, if you turned to this chapter first, hoping to get just the 1-2-3 method of housetraining and fail to read the rest of the book, which necessarily contains qualifications and further explanations, you might find the program backfiring on you. Verbal and sometimes physical discipline is acceptable for housetraining accidents but only within the context in which the dog lives and that context is different for each individual dog and owner.

# 6

# Confinement, Crates or Incarceration?

---

**I**F YOU WANT YOUR puppy or older dog to get housetrained, you simply *must* confine the dog. There is no way around it. Owners who bring the puppy or dog home and let it have the run of the house are just asking for trouble. There might be a rare dog who will be able to assume that amount of responsibility right away, but most can't. Crate or confine your puppy or dog, and allow the pet freedom only when you can directly supervise it or until the dog is truly housetrained.

Begin by confining your dog to a small area, preferably using a baby gate to keep the dog in. Get the highest gate you can find, because even the tiniest dogs learn to jump or climb—and don't get the type with diamond-shaped holes, otherwise your dog might try to get through them or may get its head stuck in the opening. The type with very small square openings is best. Often looking for a gate in a child-care shop will be more productive than looking at your local pet store. The tension-type gate is nice since you don't have to fool around with screws and mar your doorway molding.

If you have a puppy or older dog who scales the gate, try arranging it so that it tilts in toward the confinement space. Another method would be to place a foot locker or other large object underneath the gate to elevate it. Don't be at all surprised if your pet is doggedly determined to hurdle the gate. I've seen many dogs who will use the gate rungs or openings as footholds, work their way to the top, teeter there and plunge down.

Besides being dangerous, such gymnastics thwart house-training because the dog will then have more space than it can responsibly handle, and, if you are paper training, the dog will not be able to get to the papers (no, the dog will not rescale the gate to defecate in the right place). Do whatever you must to *make sure* your pet cannot escape the confined area.

Many people decide to use the bathroom or kitchen as the confinement room. Whatever choice you make, you'll have to consider several angles. First, you are going to have to step over the gate or take it down to get in or out of the room. That's a hassle, and to solve the problem some owners will invest in two medium-height gates, using one until the dog gets big enough to scale it, and then adding the other. In this way, you can step over the first gate, at least until you have to put up the second. You'll have to evaluate which room you want to gate.

Pick a room without a carpeted surface. If you are paper training, make sure that the room is large enough to separate the important functions of sleeping, eating and drinking, and eliminating. In my opinion these functions should be at least three or four feet apart, but no more than ten feet apart for an untrained dog using a confined space (food and water are one "function" and can be placed together). If you are in a tight spot with a tight space to offer Fido, and do not have enough room for a bed, eating area and toilet area, then eliminate the sleeping area. If you are not paper training, just have a sleeping and eating area, but separate them.

If you are paper training, be sure that the papers are arranged in a neat square, not just thrown down haphazardly. It makes a difference. When the papers are neatly squared and

Begin by confining your dog to a small area, using a baby gate to keep the dog in.

If you are paper training, separate the three important functions: elimination area, sleeping area and eating and drinking area.

large in area there is a "runway effect" from the dog's vantage point near the ground, clearly delineating the area for elimination. Make the papers at least five thick and overlap them. If you use absorbent pads, overlap them also. The correct size? For a small dog, at least one section of a full-sized newspaper, opened flat out; for a medium dog, two sections; and for a large dog, four. Do not use small tabloid newspapers—they will not overlap correctly, can be pushed around by the dog more easily and dislocated, and seem to invite shredding.

## Crates

If you're already upset by the "crate" heading, fearful that I am going to tell you to lock Fifi up in a crate forevermore, my advice to you is the same advice with which Joan Rivers admonishes her audiences, "Grow up!" There's *absolutely nothing wrong* with using a crate to housetrain your dog and, in fact, almost everything *right* about it. I can only offer you my own track record. Of all the dogs I've had to housebreak, the one I housebroke without a crate took twice as long.

Why, you might ask (especially if you are a professional and know about the value of crates as a training tool), didn't I mention them first? Because I am also a realist. For instance, there are many people who, even once educated about crates, will have a psychological impediment that will literally freeze their limbs when it comes time to trot Tippy to the crate. Don't ask me where this phobia comes from—but I've seen it.

Secondly, there are some instances where the area that is to be used for confinement is so small, so chew-proof and so convenient that the area is, in essence, a crate. For instance, in Manhattan, residents pay more money for less space. Kitchens and bathrooms are, in many cases, crate-size. A simple baby gate makes the area a crate. Then, too, there is the economic point that many people can afford a baby gate (or have one already) but they cannot or will not invest in a crate.

All those qualifications aside, if you want to have house-training success swiftly, just get a crate and use it. Question me now, question me while you're using it and thank me (and all the

There's absolutely nothing wrong with using a crate to housetrain your dog. It is an effective training tool.

other advanced trainers and behaviorists) later. Crates speed up the housetraining process greatly.

A little background may be helpful. The dog is a den animal. If your dog had been born in the woods, the mother and father would have found some sort of cave, den or overhang for a nursery. As you've found out, for the first three or four weeks the mother would have kept this den clean by eating all the waste materials produced by her brood. When the pups get older, she lets them know, via growls and eye contact and maybe some nudges (shoves and shakes for the slower pups), that elimination belongs outside—*not* in the crate, excuse me, den. The crate is historically valid because it mimics the den, and pups do not want to soil in their own den.

Crates come in several styles. There is the see-through variety and the plastic airline models that have a door grating in the front. I've seen some other models, mostly weird (like hooded wooden models), but stick to either of these two types. I like the plastic airline crates because they are easy to clean, can be used for travel (the see-through models will be rejected at airport counters) and you can stack items on top of them. Some owners want to be able to see their dog and have the dog see them when in the crate, but, frankly, I don't. I find that the see-through models more easily facilitate separation anxiety, stress whining and longing looks from the dog that con the owner into letting the pooch out.

If you have a crate and have been using it and your dog soils in it, it's probably too big. Get a smaller one, or lessen the space in the larger one until the dog can handle the area. This can be done by putting something large and indestructible in one half of the crate, like an ice cooler or even a cement block. The rest of the crate should be left bare, especially for a young puppy, until the pup has shown that he or she can keep the crate clean (give the pup a seven-day trial). You can then add a towel or rug for comfort. There is no sense in adding a comfort item prior to the proofing period because the pup may just defecate on it.

*Even* when the crate is the right size, there *are* dogs who will eliminate in their crates. Let's clear up this "the-pup-will-never-eliminate-in-its-den" myth once and for all. Some *will*. In researching this book I found text after text containing the flat statement that a puppy or dog will "never" eliminate in a crate, and it's just untrue. Dogs who, prior to being procured by their owners, have lived in filth (sometimes at a poorly managed shelter or pet store) will not hesitate to eliminate in a crate, no matter how much you decrease the size. They are quite used to eliminating near themselves, and will see nothing wrong with it. In these cases, it's probably better to confine the pup to the kitchen or bathroom, rather than clean out the crate and clean up the dog every day. Remember very young pups cannot be crated for longer than two to four hours, and older dogs (post-nine months) can rarely be crated longer than six to eight hours. If you are observing those guidelines and your pup consistently soils the crate, try confinement instead of crating. Forget about the books that say a dog would never do that if it was in its right mind. Soiling the crate doesn't mean the dog is crazy. It means the dog soils his crate, period, and that can have many causes. Needless to say, try another method—like confinement—but even then, avoid *incarceration*, whether you confine or crate.

## Avoiding Incarceration

Confinement and crating can be misused, especially by owners who don't want to *ever* risk the chance of an accident, or by owners who are ambiguous about having a dog in their lives and just don't want to deal with the animal. Incarceration will make your dog neurotic, but crating or confinement will help the dog to housetrain itself and avoid many other problems.

Many owners wonder how they can easily and safely let their dogs out of the crate or confinement and not have a whirling dervish racing through the house knocking over everything and everyone in sight, or a canine sneak who will saunter off and soil. The safest procedure is to *umbilical cord* the dog. The method of umbilical cording the dog first appeared in *How to Be Your Dog's Best Friend* in 1978, and it is surprising that no one thought of it beforehand (although several authors have since). I included it in the book then because it is the method that I was taught in the monastery—in fact, according to monastery rules back then, *no* puppy was to be out of its crate or confined area unless it was (1) in the appropriate area for elimination or (2) umbilical corded to you via a leash so that mistakes could be corrected immediately. That was a hard-and-fast rule and I never questioned it. You see, in a sparkling clean, orderly environment like a monastery (even one that has dogs) a housetraining accident was a sin—for the monk and the dog! I never questioned this rule (in that kind of life you don't question, you just *do)* and now I see the wisdom of the policy and would urge you to use umbilical cording also. Here's how it works.

In the first method, you simply attach the puppy's leash to your belt loop or waist and then you tell yourself, "Okay, for the next three hours (four hours, five hours, day, week, whatever time you have) I am not going to detach this dog from myself unless I am detaching it in the appropriate area for defecation or unless I have to cross a moat." I hasten to add that most moats are located in England and even then they have bridges across them. The point is: Keep the dog umbilical corded and close. You might be wondering, "But what if the dog has an accident?" My advice would be to be grateful because when a dog is umbilical corded you can correct the dog *right away* and it is manifestly clear who produced the waste matter. After all, there's only two of you there and you didn't do it. You then correct the dog using the methods described in Chapter 5.

During dinner, TV, reading or entertaining, keep the dog umbilical corded but don't hold the leash—sit on it. If you hold the leash during this time you will encourage the dog to fool around with the "give" in the leash, and you will not have both hands free to do whatever you want to do. Slip the leash under your bottom and try to trail if off to the side of the chair. Measure out only as much lead as your dog needs in order to lay down, no more. You can do this by simply pushing the dog down for a second (or giving him the down command, if he knows it) and then feeding out the appropriate amount of leash. If you give the dog too much, the dog will simply chew on it or dance around on the end of it. When your dog pulls against the dead weight of the leash, it will become quickly apparent that the object (your body) is immovable, and, like most of us do when

The Umbilical Cord Method: Attach the dog's leash to your belt loop and go about your day. You'll know exactly where your dog is and can more effectively avoid housetraining accidents.

During dinner, TV, reading or entertaining, keep the unhousebroken dog umbilical corded, but don't hold the leash—sit on it.

straining to move a heavy object, the dog will give up trying. At this point, many dogs will attempt to explore other options. These might include stress whining, chewing on the lead, jumping up on you or chewing the flooring. *Cancel all of these options through discipline.* The fact is, with this method of umbilical cording, *there are no options,* and the only acceptable response is for the dog to settle down and be quiet. If the dog stress whines, growl at the dog and make eye contact (do not whine back); if the leash is being masticated, whip it firmly up and out of the dog's mouth with a stern "No." If the dog jumps up on you, grasp the lead close to its neck area and yank down on it hard, with a "No." If the dog chews the flooring, use the swat under the chin method or the shake. Do not give the dog a toy during this period. The message is no play, no toy, no pet, *nothing.*

It is a shock for many dogs to find out that no other options are available, but most quickly adapt and do the most sensible next thing—go to sleep. It is even harder for many owners to enforce this method of umbilical cording, especially if they are used to making their dog the center of attention, catering to its every need and shoving something in its mouth every two seconds. The message, "I like you, I love you, but there are times when you must leave me alone and if you have to eliminate just hold it," will, to some owners, be emotionally wrenching.

This exercise is a wonderful housebreaking tool. It's a way to get the dog out of confinement or the crate without risking accidents that you discover later, and a great way to teach the dog to "hold it." Please remember, housetraining doesn't just mean that the dog has to learn to eliminate in the appropriate place, it also means that sometimes, life being what it is, access to that place just isn't possible and the dog just has to exercise sphincter control. Umbilical cording teaches that to the dog and is an excellent way for you to *bond* with your dog.

My toughest housetraining case was a dog I had assigned to me at the monastery. All the dogs were divided up amongst the monks and I was asked to care for Zanta, a five-year-old dog recently imported from West Germany for her excellent bloodlines. (The monastery supports itself by raising German Shepherd Dogs.)

While Zanta's genetics were great, we quickly found out that she was most definitely *not* housetrained. She was highly intelligent, in fact she held the coveted H.G.H. degree, the highest award for sheep-herding ability awarded in West Germany. However, she had always lived in a barn, eliminating when and where she desired. I started basic obedience training, transferring Zanta from German to English commands. And I immediately umbilical corded her unless she was in the desired area for elimination. At night, I tethered her to my bed with a short leash.

Zanta made a few mistakes and I was right on the other end of the umbilical cord to reprimand her. I think she had three mistakes. If a five-year old dog from Germany can clean up her act, your dog can too—it's never too late!

# 7

# Schedule or Perish!

"SCHEDULE-SCHMEDULE!" my angry client barked back at me as I lectured her for the umpteenth time on how important it was to take her Yorkie out to relieve itself at regular intervals. "I don't like to have a *schedule* for my day," she added regally. "I prefer a *plan*—so that I can shape my time to suit *me*, why can't Rascal adjust to that?" My choices at this point were to terminate the interview, get angry, throw up or educate. I chose the latter.

I patiently explained that Rascal's gastrocolic reflexes told him to urinate or defecate soon after drinking or eating. Because the little pup was only four months old, he had not developed much control and would need set times—a schedule—to eliminate. This schedule needed to be adhered to strictly until more control was developed, and then, and only then, could the dog adjust to a day "planned" in a more freelance style. I found myself moving away from using the word "schedule" with this client and using phrases like "set times" and "predictable times." People are at best funny and at worst totally neurotic. This client had a hang-up about the word "schedule." No mere *dog* was going to force her to schedule a life that she had been living for years in the most undisciplined and unscheduled way. Nor was any trainer going to bamboozle her into it. So I simply changed the semantics and set up the following schedule for her and Rascal:

**AM**

| | |
|---|---|
| 8:00 | Get up, walk Rascal immediately. |
| 8:15 | Feed and water Rascal, play with puppy. |
| 8:45 | Walk Rascal. |
| 9:00 | Bed Rascal down in crate or confined area. |
| Noon | Feed Rascal second meal. |

**PM**

| | |
|---|---|
| 12:15 | Walk Rascal. |
| 12:30 | Obedience session: come, sit stay. |
| 12:45 | Short play sessions featuring ball play. |
| 1:00 | Bed Rascal down in crate or confined area. |
| 4:00 | Kids home from school, do Round Robin Recall (pass dog around in a circle). |
| 4:30 | Feed last meal to have pup empty for overnight. |
| 5:00 | Walk Rascal. |
| 5:30 | Umbilical cord Rascal (sit on leash) for dinner. |
| 6:30 | Kids play with Rascal in confined area. |
| 7:00 | Walk Rascal for elimination, then a short run. |
| 7:30 | Put Rascal in confined area. |
| 8:00 | Offer water, then take up for night. |
| 10:30 | Walk Rascal, offer two or three teaspoons water when you return, bed dog down for night in confined area. |

This is a nifty schedule for almost any owner of a young puppy. "But all those walks!" you might say. Yes, there are six walks according to the initial schedule (or six paper pit-stops if you are paper training) and that is a lot of chances for the dog to eliminate. But your pup *needs* that many chances at first— perhaps even desperately. You will find that if you mentally note which walks the puppy chooses to use for elimination, you can cut out one, two and even eventually three of the outings on which he consistently refrains from eliminating.

However, don't start eliminating walks from the schedule until you have observed a consistent pattern for over two weeks. For instance, many dogs will not eliminate during the 5:00 PM walk, and you might be able to have the pup go the bulk of the evening "holding it" and take the pup out for the final 10:30 PM walk—or perhaps you'll find it best to move that walk to 10:00 PM. The schedule is not etched in stone—and your pup will determine certain aspects of it by his or her personal style and needs. Your needs and style will also shape the schedule— especially if you are a working owner. Here is a sample schedule for someone who works 9 to 5, Monday through Friday, owns a puppy less than five months of age, and *absolutely cannot* come home from work and cannot provide for *anyone* to come home at mid-day and allow the dog access to the desired area for elimination. This owner must use papers and must follow this schedule:

**AM**

| | |
|---|---|
| 7:00 | Get up, walk Chuckles immediately for exercise and/or elimination. |
| 7:15 | Feed Chuckles ¼ of total daily ration, during this time attend to personal care. |
| 7:50 | Walk Chuckles again for exercise and/or elimination. |
| 8:00 | Short obedience session to remind Chuckles who is Alpha. |
| 8:10 | Leave for work. Make goodbye calm. Leave moderate amount of water, and confine Chuckles in area that includes sleeping quarters, water bowl and elimination papers. Leave radio on. |

**PM**

| | |
|---|---|
| 5:30 | Return from work, greet Chuckles calmly. Release from confinement. |
| 5:45-6:00 | Feed Chuckles ¾ of ration, take up water after feeding. |
| 6:10 | Walk Chuckles for exercise and/or elimination. |
| 6:30 | Umbilical cord dog (sit on leash) while eating dinner. |
| 7:00 | Play session, include fetch. |

49

| | |
|---|---|
| 8:00 | Watch TV together. |
| 9:00 | Obedience session. |
| 9:15 | Walk Chuckles for exercise and/or defecation. |
| 9:30 | Offer small amount of water, then put Chuckles in confined area with papers. |
| 10:30- 11:00 | Retire with Chuckles on floor near bed (tether if necessary). |

If you glance over the two schedules you will find that they cover the extremes in dog-owning styles. I know that there are readers who will object to my even *outlining* a schedule for the 9-to-5 owner who leaves the dog alone for long stretches. They will say that such souls just shouldn't have a dog, period. However, I doubt that my fellow professional trainers will say that. It's reality and we've learned to respect that.

The fact is, people who work 9 to 5 every day *do* procure dogs and *do* need to be provided with a schedule. Of course, I repeat *of course*, the situation is not ideal—but it hardly borders on criminal. In the same breath, I must urge all 9-to-5 owners to try to arrange for someone to come in at mid-day and walk the dog. You'd be surprised how many trustworthy school kids would jump at the opportunity and will be very responsible about the job. The fact that the dog will probably not eliminate outdoors (the pup thinks it should go inside, on the papers) doesn't really matter—the pup still needs exercise and social interaction.

Under no circumstances should the 9-to-5 owner attempt to crate his or her puppy for that length of time. The puppy will be put in a position of having to soil the crate—the time period is simply too long. But, you can leave the crate (open the door) in the confined area and many pups will use it as a sleeping area. In fact, I've known many 9-to-5 pups who will sleep practically the whole time their owners are away, waking up only for a piddle once or twice and then sacking out again. A radio helps to mask outside noises and if kept on soft music (not rock or talk shows) can lull the pup to sleep and help wile away the time.

## Schedules Are Scribbled in Stone

Schedules are important and it is essential to have one if you want to housetrain effectively, but as I tell my clients, schedules are scribbled in stone. In stone because you *have* to have one, and scribbled because the schedule will change as the dog matures and as your own circumstances change.

For instance, as the dog matures, it might be possible to skip a walk, or sleep in on a Saturday or Sunday morning. You have to sort out the schedule yourself, often by trial and error—usually by an error on your rug! Should you discipline for such an infraction, especially when it is you who is changing the schedule? In my opinion, *yes*—although owners often refrain from reprimanding the dog because they are guilt-ridden over scrambling the schedule.

But, the fact is, housetraining doesn't mean that access to the desired area for elimination is *always* provided. As with toilet training children, sometimes access to the desired area just isn't possible—so hold it. For this reason, I would still reprimand the dog for the infraction, go back to the original schedule and try the same change later on. But remember to be fair. You can't discipline if the stool is runny, and you can't spring a foolish schedule change on a young dog—like expecting the dog to hold it for twelve hours.

A good technique in sifting out your schedule is to put yourself in the dog's place. Ask yourself how long *you* could refrain from eliminating, and then cut the figure in half—remember, the dog is a child in this area. Remember all those recess breaks the teachers gave you in first and second grade? Remember how they were cut down with every passing year of school until you were sitting through three-hour lectures in college? You were being housebroken, in case you didn't realize it. I went to Catholic school for twelve years and, believe me, the nuns did a fantastic job with me! In fact, we used to wonder when *they* took care of *their* needs!

# 8

# What Goes in Comes Out: Nutrition and Housetraining

---

I TOLD YOU EARLIER that house-training literature is full of gaps, discrepancies and contradictions. It is also full of frank cop-outs, especially in the area of nutrition. The authors I researched fastidiously stayed away from suggesting any particular food and, in fact, usually left their readers to their own devices—saying, simply, "feed a well-balanced diet" or some other elusive advice. That's what I call a cop-out. What your dog eats is intimately connected, even *centrally* connected with the success or lack of success, the speed or delays in housetraining.

This simple fact would seem obvious, but, as I noted, it is widely glossed over in the available literature. There are several reasons. First, veterinarians and trainers under contract to tout a given pet food have to suggest that particular food or at least ones that resemble it. Others worry that if they say anything against a particular kind of pet food, they will never receive the lucrative offers that can be forthcoming from companies—so saying nothing becomes more desirable than saying *anything.* Others will feed their *own* pets specialty foods but will not feel any compulsion to educate the masses as to better pet foods, or try to advise against home concoctions. A "let-them-eat cake" (or, more appropriately, soy or some other vegetable matter) attitude prevails, despite evidence that meat-meal based dry products have definite health advantages and can facilitate the housetraining process.

As for myself, I don't work for any pet food company. I never have and probably never will. I have definite *preferences* in pet foods, and I try to be as kowledgeable as I can about the whole gamut of pet food products. I had an invaluable chance to hear about the food/housetraining connection when I traveled New York and New Jersey with a veterinary nutritionist as a speaking partner. Together we gave talks on the clinical and behavioral aspects of canine nutrition. And my casework over the last fifteen years has educated me as to what works and what doesn't vis-à-vis food and the housetraining process.

We don't have the space here, and you don't have the patience to listen to a lengthy lecture on the evils of commercial food products, so I will be brief as I explain the four major types of dog foods: canned, semimoist, nonfixed-formula dry and fixed-formula specialty foods.

## Canned Foods

Here I must be blunt and frank—don't use these foods as the sole ration for your dog. You will never get the dog housetrained on these canned products and you might do great damage feeding canned foods alone. There are several problems with canned products. First, they are 65–78 percent water. The ingredients in American pet foods are listed on the label according to what makes up the food. The first or second ingredient you will see on a canned food label is water. Sometimes the company will add a nicely elusive phrase like "water sufficient for processing"—which means the amount of water was "sufficient" for that particular company. So you are paying meat prices for water, which is silly on an economic level and even more disastrous if you have a dog you are trying to housetrain. You are adding even more water into the dog's system than what the pet drinks on its own.

Since canned foods are so high in water content, they often complicate housesoiling problems such as in-house urination and territorial marking since, besides the regular supply of water, the dog has an additional source of water in the canned food.

The high levels of sodium nitrite contained in canned products can act as a diuretic in many dogs. Sodium nitrite is a color enhancer. It keeps the canned food, at best, a bright red, at worst a murky brown color so that you, the consumer, are not too turned off when you open the can. Some canine specialists say dogs have color vision; the majority say that everything is like black and white TV for dogs. Regardless of whether they do or don't see color, I sincerely doubt whether they use whatever color vision they may have to make value judgments on the color of a canned product. The coloring is strictly for consumer appeal, but harmful to the housetraining process. Further, iron oxide (another color enhancer) is nondigestible and when eliminated is concentrated—producing a deep stain on your carpet.

Perhaps the worst problem with canned foods is the meat that actually *does* manage to get into the can—taking up whatever space is not occupied by water and sodium nitrite. Dr. Wendell Belfield, a veterinarian, writes in *How to Have A Healthier Dog:*

> Animals that are rejected for human consumption are commonly used in commercial pet foods. So-called "4-D's," meaning dead, dying, diseased or disabled animals are also used for pet foods.
>
> Shocking, isn't it? The buying public hasn't got the foggiest notion that 4-D animals are used in pet foods. Do you expect the TV commercials to boast that product X uses only the finest of diseased meat? One USDA official made this comment to me: "Some of these companies claim all beef in their cans and this is true. But they don't tell you the source is a 4-D animal. Most people think they are getting sirloin steak. If they think the

55

healthiest animals in the world are going into those products, they are sadly mistaken.

Now, if you are feeding some canned food—perhaps to flavor a dry ration or as a "spike" if your dog goes off his food—I don't want you to panic. There's nothing wrong with using canned products in moderation. But I would not advise you to continue with canned products if you have been using them as the sole ration for your dog. Further, if you are experiencing any housetraining difficulties I would suggest that you eliminate any canned foods from your dog's diet, along with coat supplements, vitamins, people food and any other additives. It is my strong belief that a dog experiencing housetraining difficulties will more quickly clean up its act if fed *only* a high-quality dry ration until cleanliness and regularity are insured. More on supplements later on.

## Semimoist Foods

Semimoist products are a distinct subcategory of foods in the pet food industry. Please don't misunderstand—I'm not talking here about wetting dry food when I mention the term semimoist. Instead, semimoist foods are soft to the touch, usually come in plastic bags or plastic wrappers, are most often colored bright red and/or yellow and are usually not in pellet form but rather are molded into hamburger shape or placed in a pouch. It is the convenience of these foods that hooks many owners on them, since there is no mixing involved, no can to open, no bag to be stored.

Humans also get turned on by these foods because they are brightly colored, even shockingly red or yellow, and the package itself usually sports a photograph or sketch of a beguiling canine wolfing down the product. The red and yellow hues are meant to suggest, of course, meat or cheese. You should know that semimoist products are a poor choice for the sole ration for your dog. They can be used sparingly—never more than ¼ of the total ration—mixed with a top-quality dry food, but if you are having the slightest difficulty getting your dog housetrained, I would advise you to drop such foods from your dog's diet completely.

Semimoist foods are chocked full of sugar. Sometimes sugar is the second or third ingredient that makes up the food! These foods are also high in preservatives like BHA and BHT, and propylene glycol (also used in antifreeze), added to keep the food soft and to insure longer shelf life. Semimoist products also contain significant amounts of cereal and the sugar/cereal mixture adds up to a food with low digestibility, high stool volume and potential complications for the owner who is trying to housetrain a dog.

## Nonfixed-Formula Dry Foods

In the pet food industry, a nonfixed-formula food is a food that is usually made in large batches from ingredients that are bought on the commodities market and then stored. The formula for the food is not fixed—usually because the ingredients may vary slightly (soy grits might be used one week, soy flour another, for instance). Soy, wheat feed flour, corn gluten meal or wheat middlings are often used as the primary ingredient in dry nonfixed-formula foods. Most of the "big name" foods fall into this category. If you consult the package and look at the column that indicates how much of the food your dog is supposed to consume, you will most probably find that your dog doesn't eat that much. But the dog *is* supposed to eat that amount in order to get what is promised in the corresponding chart that details the percentages for protein, fat and other essential nutrients. It is not difficult to decipher that you are caught in a classic consumer crunch. Your dog most probably cannot eat the required bulk to get the promised amount of protein and fat. Often dry foods will contain several carbohydrates in order to make up the difference, and to insure intestinal movement. Unfortunately, with proper intestinal movement comes mountains of feces, and often mountains of *loose* feces.

High stool volume certainly doesn't help the dog that is trying to "hold it" as part of the housetraining challenge, and it certainly doesn't help the owner who must clean up feces. I prefer a fiber substance like bran or beet pulp to insure proper intestinal movement, and such substances can usually be found in the next group of foods.

### Fixed-Formula Dry Foods—"Specialty Foods"

Fixed-formula dry foods are usually foods that are made in small batches, usually with meat-meal as the primary protein source and often the predominant ingredient. The formula for the food is fixed, and the incoming ingredients are checked as they are delivered. Often quality control is more substantive, with careful ingredient selection, testing of the food as it is being made, and retention of samples of the finished product so that they can be checked in case there are consumer complaints about a given batch of food.

Most often the dog *can* eat the required amount of food to get the promised amount of nutrients. Stool volume is almost always lower, and the stools from many specialty foods are firmer. Several of these foods contain bran or beet pulp to insure proper intestinal movement. Beet pulp, for instance, can reinstate peristalsis in a dog with loose stools.

Because the dog eats less of such foods, it is extremely important to *measure* the amount of food you should be feeding until you have memorized what that amount looks like in the dog's feed dish. Remember, with specialty foods, *measure and then memorize*. Better yet, measure each day to be sure you are not overfeeding these foods. The American mentality is to over-feed—so it is often necessary to turn to the absolute impartiality of the measuring cup.

Consult the package carefully and measure the amount of food needed according to your dog's weight. Get in the habit of weighing your dog periodically (every week if you have a growing puppy) so that you can measure the amount of food correctly. Don't just "wing it"—seeing what the dog will eat—as many dogs will overeat and thus have more difficulty getting themselves housetrained. A good way to weigh your dog is to weigh yourself on a standard bathroom scale and mark down your weight on a piece of paper. Yes, I know it's hard to face that weight figure (not to mention the body figure it produces) but do it anyway! Then, cup your arms under your puppy or dog, grasp firmly and remount the scale. Look down, or better yet, have someone else check the number that now registers on the scale. Subtract your weight from that number and the difference is how much your dog weighs. Be sure to bend your knees when you lift the dog—if you throw your back out, you'll *never* get your canine companion housetrained!

## Supplements and Housetraining

If you use a good quality meat-meal based food you usually do not have to supplement your dog's ration. In fact, it is very easy to throw the formulation of some of the specialty foods out of kilter if you play with supplements. Unfortunately, adding a little bit of this and a little bit of that is a cultural mentality handed down from the time when pet foods weren't complete and needed supplementation. Breeders often advocate supplements and many send their clients home with long lists of additives—vitamins, minerals, dairy products, oils and other lotions and potions. Many breeders will turn an absolutely deaf ear to entreaties from veterinarians or canine nutritionists who suggest a good basic ration and a minimum of supplementation.

Supplement supporters aren't usually thinking along behavioral lines and, since they themselves rarely have difficulty housetraining their dogs, don't realize that not everyone is so knowledgeable and oversupplementation can easily produce loose stools and make good control difficult for the dog. Coat conditioners, for instance, can easily be withheld from the diet until the puppy is housetrained. The puppy doesn't need them if he or she is eating a good quality food, and (in most breeds) the puppy coat has to grow out naturally anyway. Oils and people foods, especially those high in fat (like steak trimmings) easily "oil up" the intestines and in many cases cause stools to "slide out" quite unexpectedly. We want to feed a high-quality food with a fiber substance (like beet pulp) that will help the puppy retain the stool, so that the pup can, on the basis of the education and discipline we give, have more time to "think out" where the stool should be placed—and if it has to be *held* until access is provided to that desired location. Why make it harder on the poor puppy or unhousetrained older dog by sprinkling and lacing the food with additives that make control more difficult?

If your breeder or pet store operator gives you a list of supplements and binds you under pain of mortal sin to use them, start asking some questions. Ask whether these supplements are necessary if you use a high-quality specialty food. Ask how these supplements will affect your housetraining progress. Ask if it is absolutely necessary to add the supplements right away or if this can wait until housetraining is accomplished.

For instance, although the jury is definitely out on the relationship between megadoses of vitamin C and hip dysplasia (a congenital ailment that plagues many larger breeds), many breeders are routinely recommending giving the vitamin. Whether or not the vitamin helps ward off hip dysplasia, we do know that it can have a diarrheic effect on many dogs, complicating the housetraining process.

Dairy products are also dangerous additives and produce runny stools in some dogs. People food should be avoided as a matter of good behavioral policy, lest the dog turn to begging at the table, but it should be especially taboo during housetraining. Dog treats that are full of preservatives or dyes (often to keep a "meat center" bright red) can also throw many dogs' innards for a loop and complicate cleanliness. My general advice is to stay away from supplements during the housetraining process and use only minimal or no additives later on—but *do* use a quality daily ration!

## Where to Feed

A method of feeding that is in my opinion highly debatable is the Grand Central Station method in which the dog's ration is placed squarely in the flow of human and/or canine traffic in the belief that the dog enjoys being fed in this fashion! I am willing to bet big bucks that this is precisely how the majority of American dogs eat.

I have prostrated myself flat on the floor in such households, about six to ten feet from the eating dog, and made observations I was never able to make from above. Dogs often lift their eyes anxiously, stop eating and trail—with their eyes—human feet that trespass too close. They may bolt their food, or snarl sometimes inaudibly. Meanwhile humans stroll about gleefully thinking how nice it is that Fido is part of the happy family and eats right with the others. The fact that the dog is a pack animal that instinctively guards its food doesn't seem to dawn even on some experienced dog people.

The Grand Central Station approach is an insult to a dog on a rational and genetic level. We know that stress, nutrition, training and care are intimately connected, and if what I've described isn't a stressful eating arrangement I'd like to know what is.

Feed your dog alone in a room, or in a crate—let him or her enjoy the preferably twice-daily ration in peace. How many times have you been dissatisfied at a restaurant because your table was in the flow of heavy traffic? Perhaps the distraction even made you angry or unable to digest your food. Let your dog enjoy his daily bread without dread.

Owners will often complain to me that the dog will consume its food and immediately run off and have an accident. I've had many owners insist that *as the dog is eating,* defecation and/or urination is occurring at the other end of the body. I've never seen this particular phenomenon, and I think it is probably owner hyperbole (usually provided to impress the trainer with the urgency of doing something *now* about the problem—or, worse yet, cast the dog in the role of a complete idiot that defecates as it eats). If I do observe this syndrome, I'll retract these comments but I'm willing to bet that most dogs wait at least thirty seconds before eliminating after eating—and more likely it is fifteen to thirty minutes.

Whatever the case, where you feed has a lot to do with whether the dog can sneak off and lay a load. If the dog is in a room, left alone with the food, you'll return and find the accident right away. And if the dog is in the crate, there's even less of a chance that an accident will happen. But if the dog is eating in the kitchen as you sleepily drink your coffee, a quick exit and a quick excretion is much more possible and the "sneak exit" can become patterned in. All of this can be avoided if you feed your dog in a small confined room or in the crate.

Finally, if you feed in the presence of other people, the dog is more likely to focus on you and the others in the room and not eat all of the ration right away. This leads to the nibbler syndrome, which is a disaster when you are trying to get the dog housebroken. It also increases the chance that the owner will be there to coax or cajole the dog into eating, leading to another whole host of behavioral difficulties. Others might take pity on the dog and share table scraps, teaching the dog to focus on the family table rather than the food bowl. The dog can't do that if he's not fed Grand Central Station style.

## When to Feed

Times of feedings will vary according to the dog's age and the schedule you have set up for the dog (see Chapter 7). But whatever schedule you follow, it is always best to keep your dog on two meals a day, adjusting the amount of food served at each feeding according to the intake you want the dog to have to insure housetraining success. Two meals a day help to relieve hunger tension. There is a center in your dog's brain called the hypothalamus. If the hypothalamus acts up, so does the dog. If there is hunger tension, there is more chance of bad behavior.

The hypothalamus is extremely delicate, and the dog never really masters complete control over it (humans have a hypothalamus too, and we are expected to gain control of it, but most of us don't). The hypothalamus regulates temperature and appetite, and unless it is kept satisfied, naughty behavior is more of a possibility—especially stress-related behavior.

This is one area in which legitimate comparison can be made between the behavior of dogs and the behavior of children in general. If your kid or your dog is hungry you stand a higher risk of bad behavior. To keep the hypothalamus satisfied, it might be necessary, for some dogs, to feed two times a day, during the dog's waking periods. This has a calming, resting effect and helps to stabilize bad behavior. Remember also that if the dog's stomach is empty he may attempt to drink more water to "fill up" the gap—thus increasing the chance of urination accidents.

The feedings are best placed in the early morning and early

afternoon—if you have a normal 8-to-5 working schedule. You might have to change the schedule somewhat but the important point is to keep food in the dog's stomach during its waking hours—the exception being the dog who will not have access to a proper elimination area.

## How to Feed

If, because of schedule differences, I leave you a little vague on *when* to feed your dog, I can be crystal clear about *how* to feed your dog: *never free feed your dog unless directly ordered to do so by a veterinarian.* Free-feeding, a method in which the food is simply placed out and the dog allowed to ingest it at will, is bad biochemically and behaviorally.

First, the biochemical reasons. When presented with a large bulk of food that *the dog knows will only be there for a given amount of time,* a dog will produce large amounts of saliva and eat the food quickly. Although no digestive enzymes are secreted in the dog's saliva, the saliva helps to break the food down slightly, easing work on the gut and in fact triggering digestive enzymes there. If a dog free-feeds, eating a kibble here and a kibble there, much less saliva is produced and the gut has to break down the food without the help of heavy chewing and adequate salivating. You are, in essence, forcing your dog's gut to work harder.

Behaviorally, free-feeding is the source of many problems. If you free-feed and your dog takes in the food all day long, I can almost promise you it will *come out* all day long—all over your house. The simple fact is, what goes in comes out. If you offer your dog's food in a lump sum, it will be deposited pretty much in a lump sum. That makes it much more easy to predict when to allow the dog access to a desired area.

Free-feeding is also a bad idea behaviorally because placing the food down and then picking it up—regardless of whether the dog has finished or not—makes you look *Alpha.* Even picking up the empty food dish makes you look like the leader because it reiterates the fact that *you* are the one who gives and takes back the food. Owners who free-feed are denying themselves a subtle advantage over their dogs. Finally, dogs who pick and nibble deprive themselves of the teeth-cleaning function of

63

many harder kibbles, and, in fact, many free-feeders never really fill up at all—and remain in a state of nervous anxiety. Since the food is *always* there many forget to chow-down, simply thinking, "well, it'll be there when I need it." It's like the human anorexic who keeps a full refrigerator.

My advice to owners is always the same, unless for health reasons (and this is extremely rare) a veterinarian advises otherwise: Place the food down and leave it for 10-15 minutes. Leave the dog and the food *alone* in a *quiet* room. Then, return and pick up the food even if the dog has not finished. Do not congratulate the dog if he finished and do not scold him if he did not finish. SAY NOTHING. Re-enter the room and pick up the dish, period. Never add anything to the food and re-offer it in order to get the dog to eat. Simply pick up the dish silently and re-offer that same ration (or, if it is not fresh, a new ration) at the next scheduled feeding.

### Excuses for Excuses for Excuses

The above advice might seem ultra-simple but it is precisely at this juncture that worried owners will offer a thousand "buts" and other qualifications. Let's list some of the most common here:

*But what if he doesn't eat for (one, two, three, four) days?*

Chances are, he will, if you adhere to this plan and do not cajole the dog to eat. A dog can go three or four days without eating and survive, as long as water is available. You might, indeed, have trouble switching a free-feeder over to set meals, but it is in the dog's best interest that you do so.

*Can't I just add a little steak (lamb, fat, bacon grease, truffles, filet mignon, caviar) to the food if he doesn't eat to get him going?*

No! Of course adding something yummy gets the dog to eat more quickly. But it also makes you look like a whimp, demotes you to littermate status and doesn't aid you in your housetraining goal. You are setting a trap for yourself and for your dog.

My client stared at me confidently. "There's no way you're going to get this dog to eat," she declared. "I've already tried

64

everything." I stared back confidently knowing that what was to come was so old to me I could have set it to music a long time ago.

Predictably, my client described her efforts to get Konrad to eat. She had tried every commercial food available. She had tried burger-type, semimoist products ("He threw up on those"), canned foods ("He got the runs on those") and finally people food ("Now I have a combination of the runs and throwing up—depending on his mood, I guess").

We looked into the situation more and discovered that the owner had been placing the dog's food down, waiting ten to twenty minutes and then adding something "good" when the dog wouldn't eat. This ruse lasted about six months and the dog faithfully waited for mommy to put something "yummy" in his food. The dog knew the words "mommy" and "yummy" meant to remain seated in front of the food bowl and adopt a dour, lifeless expression.

"Eat your food or mommy will have to put something yummy in it," was the dog's training phrase. The owner had, in essence, unintentionally trained the dog not to eat his food. Or, more appropriately, the dog had trained the owner to add that something "yummy."

The solution was to place Konrad alone with his prepared food in a room and give him ten minutes to eat. If within that time nothing was consumed, the owner simply picked up the food unceremoniously, neither scolding the dog for not eating nor pleading with it to eat. The same food was reoffered later in the day, again with the dog alone in a room free of distractions and set down for only ten minutes. Within two days the dog figured out the new system—that was the way feeding was conducted now, and I might as well eat up, pronto, was his reasoning.

As might be expected, the greatest problem was in getting the owner to leave the dog alone with his food and not add anything to it after it was set down. "Oh, he can't eat unless I'm there," the owner said flatly. But within two days on our system the dog was eating a properly balanced dog food and greatly enjoying it (and, probably, the new found peace experienced in being allowed to enjoy a meal alone without "mommy" hovering over him). To be sure it was a blow to "mommy's" ego and her

65

misguided instincts. She equated food with love, her presence with security for the dog, and was unintentionally wrecking the dog's health in the process.

My advice concerning finicky eaters is almost always the same. Put the dog and its food alone in a room for ten minutes and leave. Return and pick up whatever food the dog has not consumed. The only exception is if the dog is in the process of eating when you come into the room. You should then give it another five minutes to finish. Strict? Not in my book. This method is a way of undoing months and even years of unintentional training for dietary troubles.

*I tried your method for correcting the finicky eater and it didn't work. Now what?*

Frankly, in fifteen years of counseling dog owners I haven't seen a dog who wouldn't eat using the above method. Owners who say they've tried it are usually still whining—even if they are literally not saying *anything*. The owner's *eyes* look worried, the body language is tense and the dog picks up the cues and refuses to eat. This is especially true of secondhand dogs (from a shelter or another source) who may have had a series of worry-warts and whimps as owners, so that the placating behavior—and subsequent refusal to eat and/or fear of the food—is truly patterned.

If the above method has been faithfully adhered to, take the dog to your veterinarian for a full checkup, even if this has already been done. Get a second opinion if necessary. It might also be necessary to remove yourself from the feeding process altogether.

If you have a chronic food refuser, a stay at a boarding kennel that follows the above method might be of help to your dog. The presence of other dogs eating sometimes helps the finicky eater. Your dog can be placed between or near other dogs who are ravenously devouring their ration—often because they know they have only a set time with it.

*Why all this strictness about feeding? Why not just add something good to the dog's food? C'mon, you're a trainer, let us in on the secret concoctions that get finicky eaters to eat.*

I prefer working on this problem on a behavioral level rather than suggesting secret concoctions that guarantee that the dog will eat. Usually the unenlightened owner will simply abuse the new additives in the same way as the old additives the dog is now refusing. If, however, the above method of feeding is being faithfully adhered to, some "spurs" are helpful to encourage the finicky eater.

Beef broth works for many dogs, as does chicken bouillon with garlic added (both should be poured over the dog food). Various food companies make products designed for finicky eaters, usually containing garlic or beef and chicken.

Frankly, few dogs will turn up their noses at foods that are high in protein and made of meat-meal base. So don't give up on the dog that won't eat. Remember that dogs do not respond to what I call "placating" behavior—the owner who whines at his or her dog to finish its food. To the dog this whining is paralanguage that sounds like the whimper of its littermates when they refused to eat or for some reason didn't like what was offered. If your paralanguage (whining, whimpering tonalities) indicates to the dog that you are distressed over the food (C'mon, eat, pleeeeeeze) the dog could think there is something definitely wrong with the food and will refuse to taste it until you (a fellow littermate) do—which, of course, you won't! So, it's into the trash can with that load of food, which of course confirms to the dog (if he sees you toss it out, which most do) that, truly, that was a food that shouldn't have been eaten.

If you've gathered anything from this chapter, it is that nutrition, housetraining and care are a mixture in your dog's life. You have to concoct the right blend for your best friend.

# 9

# A Quick Review

**I**T MIGHT BE GOOD to pause here and briefly summarize what we have learned so far. Ask yourself the following questions:

Have you taken time to establish yourself as Alpha by practicing eye contact?

Are you using *natural* (bitch-like) corrections? Use a low, serious tone of voice to mimic the bitch's growl, a shake or a swat— no yelling, screaming or overly harsh physical discipline.

Are you following the numbered plan outlined in Chapter 5, "Specific Corrections for Housesoiling"? If you are unclear, memorize the plan again and even act it out without your dog.

Are you honestly using some method of confinement? You must use either a crate, a single room or the umbilical cord methods or a combination of all three if you are to get the dog housetrained.

Have you set up a schedule for your dog and are you following it religiously? If the schedule is not working, have you thought it out from the dog's point of view?

Are you feeding the dog decently? Have you eliminated dairy
products, coat conditioners and all treats in order to get the
dog housetrained? Check back in Chapter 8 for details on
good nutrition.

Remember the ACCESS plan:
    Alpha
    Corrections
    Confinement
    Establish
    Schedules
    Select a good food

# 10

# Eliciting
# Elimination

---

**I**T'S ONE THING to get your pooch to eliminate in the right place, it's another to get the dog to eliminate *on command*. But there are ways that you can elicit elimination by working on your pet psychologically.

While there are several methods, each with their own flourish, all of them go back to basic principles established by the Russian physiologist Ivan Pavlov (1849–1936). Pavlov is often classified as an experimental psychologist but he was actually a physiologist who just happened to experiment in psychology, perception and learning. Pavlov won the Nobel Prize in 1904 for his studies of digestion, which of course is intimately connected with elimination. Elimination can be viewed as the final step in the digestive process. Naturally, since in housetraining we are concerned with what we put into our pet and precisely when and where it comes out, Pavlov has much insight to share with us. Pavlov might be called the patron saint of anyone trying to housetrain a dog!

One technique that is highly Pavlovian in style was introduced by Dr. M. L. Smith in a nifty book sporting the no-frills title, *Eliminate on Command* (Masterworks Press). It is a positive shaping technique that won kudos from me when I reviewed the book in my *Dog Fancy* book review column. Dr. Smith doesn't claim that the method is original, in fact she states that many owners may have been using it for years without knowing it.

Dr. Smith says: "You can establish a conditioned reflex in your dog by associating a special sound with the beginning of both urination and defecation. Fifty to seventy-five repetitions are needed in order to establish a functional result. When the repetitions have been adequately carried out, the sound itself will cause the dog to 'feel an urge' and respond by eliminating anything contained in its bladder or bowel at the moment." Dr. Smith notes that from then on, any time you say the trigger word or phrase, the dog will do its best to evacuate its bladder or bowel pronto. Key phrases that are suggested are "Do it," "Sis-boom" or "Hit-it!" I like these phrases but I prefer phrases that can be said on the street without undue embarrassment. For this reason, I feel that the specter of an owner repeating, "Hit it, hit it!" to the dog might be amusing and even offensive to passersby. They might think it is a command to bite. I prefer the phrase "Do your business," since it can be said repeatedly at a quick pace, doesn't offend anyone and yet still makes it abundantly clear what is being asked. I dislike phrases that employ cutesy words or that focus on the actual substance being produced like, "Let's do a wee-wee" or "Do a crap." Worse yet are obscenities that include slang terms for fecal matter or urination.

Sometimes owners will use familiar phrases like "Get going," "Hurry up" or "C'mon." But these can be inadequate since they are part of ordinary everyday discourse, and can give the dog unintended signals if uttered at the wrong time or place. Select a phrase that is short, succinct and not something that can only be said privately, as there will be many occasions when you will have to use the phrase in front of others.

There is a pattern that most dogs follow when they get ready to eliminate. This pattern usually includes some nose grazing, some circling and some heavy sniffing or even snorting.

72

Some dogs will skip one part of the pattern or substitute whirling around for circling, sniffing the air for sniffing the ground, or some other individual flourish. Whatever the individual dog's idosyncracies, the moment when the dog will squat and begin to urinate or defecate usually becomes known and sequenced to the owner. When the haunch or squat occurs you begin your "chant." As many times as possible, repeat the key phrase and a praise phrase, softly and quickly. When the dog is no longer squatting or haunched over, stop talking, don't say anything more. We want the dog to identify the key phrase and praise with *that* specific action. Don't call the dog to you after elimination and praise it—the dog will take the praise for coming when called, not for eliminating, although it will certainly *look* like the praise is accepted for that. And don't under any circumstances offer food after calling the dog to you—again the dog will take the food and/or praise for coming. Using food is a poor way to teach the recall—even if you think you are teaching something else!

Some behaviorists say to stop praising and saying the trigger phrase *before* the dog is actually eliminating. These observers prefer that the key phrase be used just while the dog is *trying* to eliminate. But I've found that most owners aren't observant enough to get in the number of repetitions necessary to elicit elimination in that short period of time, and using the key phrase and the praise right through to closure of the sphincter muscle is quite satisfactory.

Just be sure to use the key phrase *softly* and don't use the dog's name, otherwise the dog will direct its attention to you and not to the action occurring. A substitute for using a phrase might be the sound of keys jingling—the technique of imprinting this sound onto the dog would be the same—and if you are unable to speak to your dog, you might try this as a substitute method.

Don't use this method until the puppy is at least eight weeks of age. Be sure you take the dog to the same place for elimination each time. And be sure the dog has something in him *to* eliminate before you attempt to elicit elimination. The technique won't work if you consistently coax an "empty" dog.

As soon as you've repeated your key phrase for more than one week (during at least 21 eliminations), try sitting your dog at the door, making eye contact, animating the dog and issuing the phrase. Then, scoot the dog out to the desired location. If you catch the dog near the door, circling or stress whining, deliver your key phrase in a questioning (not a whining) tone of voice and give the dog access to the desired area for elimination.

Watch out for high-powered praise when the dog is eliminating. Some owners start to scream and shriek from joy and of course the dog just stops eliminating and runs to the owner. I had one client recently who was having a considerable problem with housetraining and had one or two instances when the dog finally *did* make it to the paper. Believe it or not, after whooping it up at the top of her lungs, she and her husband ran to the refrigerator, took out a bottle of champagne (I do not know if they had been saving it for the occasion), uncorked it and drank it down gleefully while congratulating the dog.

The dog sat nearby with a totally puzzled expression on his face. Two days later, the dog defecated on the rug and instead of a champagne party he got corked. There's every possibility that the praise was too exuberant, and the dog decided to leave another load in full view of the owners in order to get some more. Keep your praise *or* scoldings concerning housetraining low-key and modulated. You don't want your dog to think that every time he manages to eliminate in the right place it is a major event for which he will be praised to high heaven. *Do* praise, but don't go overboard—or you might wind up with a dog that misinterprets and tries to "please" you by eliminating anyplace.

# 11

# Discipline
# After the Fact

In RESEARCHING THIS BOOK I
spent days at the American Kennel Club library, pouring over
various chapters on housetraining, comparing techniques and
approaches. I found that most authors simply dismissed the idea
that a dog can be disciplined for a housetraining accident after
the fact, advising clients to reprimand the dog only if it was
caught in the act. Other books prescribed various time periods
(anywhere from thirty seconds to five minutes) within which a
dog could be reprimanded for a mistake, but even these authors
hedged and said it was better to not discipline after the fact.

Of course, these authors are rightfully concerned about the
possible negative side effects stemming from discipline after the
fact, but this concern is somewhat unrealistic. It *is* better to
discipline the puppy only if caught in the act of eliminating, but
it is a rare owner who is going to be hovering over the dog
constantly in order to be right there to reprimand. No matter
how vigilant the owner is, sooner or later an accident will occur
that will be discovered after some time has passed.

I *did* find two authors who indicated that discipline after the fact is okay—under some circumstances. Carol Lea Benjamin, for instance, says that discipline after the fact is acceptable because you have "evidence" in the form of the dog's elimination (*Dog Problems*, Doubleday, 1984). Her concept of "evidence" as a spur for the dog's memory, thus providing a legitimate basis for discipline after the fact, resonated with my own experience at New Skete Monastery. There, if we came upon evidence of a mistake, and could match the appropriate dog to the evidence, we *did* discipline after the fact. Although it flew in the face of the bulk of printed information, it certainly seemed to work. The offending dog definitely seemed to get the connection between the mistake and itself, if the dog was taken quietly to the evidence, shown it, given a slight shake by the scruff and then trotted out to the appropriate area for elimination. I have found that carefully structured discipline after the fact is a workable option for *some* owners and *some* dogs.

Behaviorists and others who take a strict, linear view of canine memory capacities usually observe that a dog cannot remember doing something much later than two or three minutes after performing the act. Various "tests" are usually hauled out to substantiate this line of reasoning, usually evaluations collected in laboratory settings where the dog just doesn't function as it does in a household environment. The suggestion that dogs can understand discipline after the fact if "evidence" is available is dismissed as "anecdotal" or even invalid. But is it possible that we have sold many dogs short in this area? It *is* true that a dog lives in the here and now and that a reprimand is best issued as the crime is committed. But, as Carol Benjamin notes, there are ways of making the "then" *now*, by using the evidence to convict the dog and give it a correction with a connection. Is it possible that we have seriously underestimated our dogs in terms of what they can and can't remember?

There are some instances where discipline after the fact should never be applied:

1. If there has been a persistent pattern of the owner coming home and screaming at the dog for having accidents—reacting *to* the evidence before getting the dog *to* the evidence (see below).

2. If the puppy is very young, pre-four months of age, and no attempt has been made to confine the pup or housetrain it using nonphysical methods.
3. If the dog is older and geriatric and not capable of bladder or sphincter control any longer. There are medications that can help older dogs.
4. If the dog is in poor health.

Some trainers who believe that discipline after the fact works (and frankly quite a few do—but hardly any will put it into print) also add (again privately) that some of the "smarter" breeds seem to respond to discipline after the fact more than "slower" breeds. In other words, is it possible that comprehension of discipline after the fact is breed-specific? This opens up another area of controversy.

Any time you start talking about one breed being smart and another breed being slow, you'd better duck for cover, so I won't try to address this question here. Then, too, individuals *within* a given breed can be smart or slow, fast or dumb, idiots or Einsteins. It was curious to me, however, that the monastery Shepherds caught on to the idea of discipline after the fact so quickly and so consistently.

You don't have to be a lawyer to figure out how to handle "evidence" in order to convict the dog of a housetraining crime. The cardinal rule is: *Don't react to the evidence until you get the dog to the evidence!* Here's how it works.

You come home and the dog is in the living room five feet from the evidence, or for that matter in another room twenty-five feet from it. You, upon sighting the evidence angrily scream, "Goshdarn you Tippy, you brat, look what you've done to the new rug from Bloomies!" Worse yet, you engage in littermate stress whining, "Goshdarn yooo, Tippieeee! Look what you've done to my new rug from Bloooooommieeeeees!" (remember the chapter on paralanguage). The dog, of course, hightails it away from you. The dog may tuck its tail between its legs as it scampers away, or it may lower its eyes and roll over submissively or it may stress-defecate or submissively urinate right there on the spot. Whatever the reaction, the uneducated owner will surmise that, clearly, the dog *knows* that it has "done wrong." "He *knows* when he's done wrong; you should *see* how he looks" is a statement I hear frequently. I must say bluntly, my dear owner, *you are wrong*. It is *not* safe to presume that the dog knows specifically what it did "wrong." The dog simply knows *something* is wrong. All the dog is doing is running away from your ugly paralanguage and even uglier body language and overall presentation of yourself. The dog is *not*, repeat *not* thinking about the "evidence" because no connection has been made for the dog *with* the evidence.

But, something very sad *has* happened—the owner has screamed, shrieked, shouted or screeched at the "evidence" and the dog has run away. As the dog runs away, it says, "Oh my God, he's back again, and mad. I wonder what it is? I wonder who did it? Well, I know paralanguage and body language and I'm no fool, I'm not sticking around to find out! I'll just dive under the bed until this thing blows over, *whatever* it is."

If this episode happens often enough an even worse set of associations develops in the dog's mind. As the owner repeatedly comes home (or in from another room) and sees "evidence" and screams or whines at it, the dog comes to associate the owner's *coming home* with the distinct possibility of getting hell. The dog reasons, "Gosh, it's strange living here. Sometimes he comes home and he's nice to me. Other times he comes home and he's mean to me, and *I don't know why.*" At this point, the dog starts to live in fear, doubt and anxiety, and unless confined or crated will defecate or urinate *more* out of frustration and worry. So if you have been coming home and screaming at evidence repeatedly, you have already cashed in your chips concerning this chapter— you *cannot* discipline after the fact. The fact is, even if you've only raised the roof when you've seen evidence three or four times, you've probably set up a bad pattern in the dog's mind. My advice to you is to crate or confine your pet until housetraining success is achieved. If you continue to react to evidence, or not react and then discipline, you will simply fry your dog's brain and totally confuse him or her. You may never get the dog housebroken. In these cases, crating and/or confinement is absolutely necessary and there should be no discipline after the fact. I will hasten to add that in my experience this eliminates 50 percent of owners from ever disciplining after the fact. You just can't. Confinement, crating, proper nutrition, prevention of accidents and discipline *as the act occurs* must be the route for owners who have abused evidence.

Let me also add that if you have bungled the use of evidence, it's no reason to castigate yourself. Most owners do, naturally. It's quite normal, from a human point of view, to come home from work, enter your home or apartment, see a mess and scream bloody murder. It's also quite understandable that when the dog runs away, the owner (who of course *wants* the dog to see a connection and has a high stake at getting the dog to make one) thinks that the dog truly knows that it has "done wrong." It's also quite normal that the owner who repeats this episode time and again comes to think that the dog is acting out of spite or even that the dog is an adversary and "out to get me." Yes, friends, it's all very understandable and normal, *from a human point of view*. But dogs aren't human (who would keep them if they were, you might ask), they're dogs. Paralanguage and body language mean one thing to us, quite a different thing to them. If you ask the dog to make the leap and understand (or tolerate) you on the human level, on the level of *your* paralanguage, *your* body language, you're really being quite silly and even selfish. First, you're ignoring the fact that the two of you belong to two different species. The fact that you are both mammals and can bond with each other are the main features you share. Everything else has to be learned, on both sides.

If, on the other hand, you haven't blown your chance to discipline after the fact, be sure to do it right. Here is an outline:

1. Don't react to the evidence. Control yourself. Don't say *anything*. If the dog is in the room and you enter, avert your glance from the evidence as soon as you notice it. Even if the dog is already running away (that might be a sign that you've cashed in your chips on using discipline after the fact), don't say *anything*.
2. Go and get the dog. Some dogs will still shiver, shake or freak out as you approach because subtle body language cues are hard to disguise. Sometimes sidestepping toward the dog helps. Approach quietly. Don't say anything.

3. Get the dog's collar and bring him to the evidence, *quietly* but firmly. Sit him in front of the accident. *Don't say anything!*

4. Keep some upward tension on the collar to keep the dog in the sit position. Focus the dog's eyes on the accident. *Do not put the dog's nose in the refuse,* but do firmly orient the dog's head down toward the elimination. Don't yell, and don't whine. Keep your voice flat and deep. Growl. Focus the dog for just two to three seconds on the mess.

5. After letting the dog raise his head, give a strong tap under the chin or a firm shake under the neck as described in the chapter on discipline techniques, continue scolding and, taking the dog's collar, march the dog to the appropriate place for elimination. *Do not pick the dog up to take him to this area.* If you do, the message may be decoded by the dog as, "I do not have to use this area, even if they get mad, unless my Alpha figure(s) *pick me up and put me in this area.*" That, of course, is not the message you want to convey. The message is, "You take your four feet and go to the area or near it," so don't pick the dog up at this point.

6. If you must put the dog into a back yard, don't just push him out, *take him out* and then leave. If you have to take the dog down an elevator and onto the street, do it as quickly as possible and give the dog a slight scolding (not nagging) as you exit. If you are taking the dog to paper, rap on the paper saying, "Here! This is where you go!" in a low, firm voice, and leave the dog there. You will find that you only have to stay two or three minutes in the area you have escorted the dog to. First, the dog will be so shook up that he or she will probably not eliminate (the dog just went in the wrong place, so he might be empty) but you have to make the connection for him as to where he is *supposed* to go.

7. Make the transition from inappropriate area to appropriate area as swift and smooth as possible. Obviously, you'll be aided if the distance to be covered is short, hindered if covering that distance involves walking a long way, taking an elevator, etc.

The X marks the spot of the accident. Quietly bring the dog to the scene of the crime and, after focusing his attention on the mess, give a strong tap under the chin.

Immediately march the dog to the appropriate area for elimination. Make the transition from inappropriate area to appropriate area as swift and smooth as possible.

8. When you return, isolate the dog for at least fifteen minutes, and, if someone has not taken care of the chore yet, clean up after the dog using a 50-50 solution of white vinegar and water. Don't let the dog see you clean up—he or she shouldn't be able to, as they'll be isolated. The only exception is if you are paper training and the dog misses the paper by a wide margin. You then have to discipline, take the dog to the paper, and then turn and clean up. Even in this instance, try to turn your back to the dog and make the clean-up swift.

9. After fifteen to thirty minutes, let the dog have some freedom (unless he's being confined as a matter of general training) and be friendly, but not overbearing with the dog. Don't try to make up your guilt over disciplining the dog by coddling him at this point. You did what was proper and what the dog's own mother would have done if confronted with such a situation. You have nothing to be ashamed of, nor does the dog. The correction has been made and the episode is over. This should be your attitude. Any extremes of overbearance or continued nagging will simply confuse the dog.

# 12

# Submissive Urination

$\mathbf{W}$HEN A DOG IS urinating inappropriately, it doesn't necessarily mean that the dog has fallen off the wagon and is piddling because it is pouting—it might be afraid. Submissive urination occurs when the dog is in a state of high anxiety and feels that the owner is dominant. The urination might even be a sign of "respect" for the dominant one since squatting and marking are common signs of fealty between submissive and dominant wolves. Since the problem results from use of urine as a sign of submission, it should not be dealt with in the same way as purposeful urination. The reaction is often beyond the dog's control. In most cases, it will go away in time but there are several things you can do to hasten that day.

First, don't punish the dog. If you do, you will make the puppy or dog feel your dominance and thus it will be more anxious and more willing to "please" you by urinating even more. Instead, this type of urination is best eliminated by prevention rather than correction.

In my experience, the most frequent times submissive urination occurs are:

- When the owner arrives home and greets the dog
- When the owner reprimands the dog
- When the owner catches the dog after a chase
- When the owner argues with another human
- When friends greet the dog after coming on the owner's territory

To restructure these situations, sit down for a minute and map out some alternatives for yourself. While it is quite natural for an owner to greet a dog super-affectionately upon arriving home, the dog that submissively urinates cannot take this kind of greeting. Instead, enter the home or apartment quietly and softly greet the dog. Just a "Hello, Rascal" is all you should say. *Don't touch the dog.* Look over the dog not at it, and get busy doing something—putting your briefcase away, setting the table or hanging up your coat. Of course the dog will be cavorting around happy to see you, but as long as you do not touch him and greet him briefly and then keep moving, there is less chance that the dog will present himself in front of you, make eye contact and urinate. It is interesting to note that most dogs who engage in this behavior do so while stationed sitting in front of their owners or others, eyeball to eyeball with the human, rarely from a side position.

If you have to reprimand a dog with this problem, go quietly to the dog's side and then reprimand softly. Often, the dog that submissively urinates has to be trotted to tile flooring (or some other surface that can be cleaned easily) and *then* reprimanded. Instead of chasing the dog through the house, umbilical cord the dog to you or close off the house in advance in anticipation of chase scenes. You will then be able to short-circuit the chase.

I have never seen human arguments listed in dog training texts as a cause of submissive urination, but in my experience they often are. I have had many clients who disagree with each other concerning the handling of the dog battle out their differences in front of the dog. Often they pepper their diatribes against each other with the dog's name. The dog then hears harsh, strident, growl-like tonalities (the dog doesn't understand the English) with its own name periodically inserted. "Grrrrr, grrrrr Rascal, grrrrrr, grrrrr, grrrrrrrrr, *Rascal.*" The dog *does* know his name. "They must be talking about *me,*" the poor dog reasons, "and it's not nice—it sounds like the way my mother used to growl." Then to please the owners, the dog sneaks off to the bedroom and urinates out of tension in a hopeless quest to please its owners.

Of course, when one member of the couple comes upon the urination it provides still another reason to berate the dog (and the other half of the couple), and the vicious cycle continues. The solution, of course, is to train the dog under the guidance of a professional, either by hiring a private trainer or going to class. The disagreeing parties can then stop fighting with each other and query the trainer for sound advice. The tension level will go down and the dog will relax. The dog will gain confidence from the obedience training.

Instruct strangers and friends *in advance* not to touch your dog upon arrival if it is prone to submissive urination. If the problem is pronounced, put the dog in another room and bring the dog out for a greeting on leash. If the dog still urinates, bring the dog out on leash and place it on a down-stay. Remember, any eyeball-to-eyeball contact increases your chances that the dog will squat and squirt. Many owners teach the stand-stay to such dogs simply because it is less likely that the dog will urinate while standing. Remember, submissive urination always involves squatting and is more common in adult females than males. If a dog lifts his leg on you or your guests this is most definitely *not* submissive urination, no matter how "submissive" the dog is in other aspects.

Since submissive urination is tied to dominance and submissive patterns that are often too complex for an owner to decipher, it might be necessary to employ a trainer to eliminate the trait. The trainer is likely to recommend obedience training and you are likely to object, "I don't need obedience training, I need the dog to stop wetting in my house every time I come home" (or chase him, or shout or argue, etc.). You might feel that such advice is wide of the mark and not connected with the problem at hand—or underfoot, as the case may be.

I can assure you that the trainer's advice is correct. The trainer is trying to break the unsettling pattern of dominant human/submissive dog that has resulted in an abnormal reaction to what should be a normal human/dog arrangement. To do this, it might be necessary for you to work with your dog as a *team*, on a neutral activity that will increase the dog's confidence, allow you to praise good behavior, release tension for both of you and still allow you to maintain your necessary role as pack leader.

Remember that dogs who submissively urinate are often unaware that they are doing so. Nevertheless, while you cannot discipline the behavior, you can try to dry the dog out—without dehydrating it. Arrange a coming-home incident when the dog has been without water for some time. When you return instead of not looking at the dog at all, cast one glance its way and touch just *one finger* to its forehead, then, get busy. Watch your paralanguage too—no stressed or whiney or anxious tonalities! See what happens. Chances are, you'll find that Fido forgot to flip the faucet, and that's *one time* that the dog greeted you without making a mistake. The next day, arrange a second such "success" and likewise for day three. Gradually increase your physical contact and the amount of water you allow Submissive Sam to swill. Nothing succeeds like success, even if you have to plan successes for your dog.

Finally, if the problem is really chronic, and you have tried set-ups, training, staging successes and everything else you can think of, a stay at a boarding kennel might, repeat *might* help the dog to break the pattern. Here, there will be no dramatic hellos and goodbyes, no arguments, no strangers to greet and no anguished cries of frustration (surfaces in boarding kennels are easily cleaned). The chronic dog might just have to literally "get it all out of his system" and might need a break from the current scene. But this is only a last resort, to be taken after all the other advice I've given fails—a rare event. If you decide to use this technique first, because you are too busy, too frustrated or too angry to try the aforementioned methods, I can promise you a dog who will still submissively squat, and, of course, a whopping boarding bill.

# 13

# Leg Lifting

---

Leg LIFTING IS A particularly ob-
noxious habit that occurs in males. It's one thing to have your
linoleum floor urinated on—that can be cleaned—it's another
thing to have the sides of your furniture anointed daily. I once
had a client who had covered the sides of everything—I mean
*everything*—in her apartment. The walls were covered with
plastic up to the three-foot level. The furniture was covered
with plastic she had painstakingly sewn on. Table legs were
wrapped in tin foil, and a floor-level birdcage was surrounded by
(this is the truth) barbed wire, because the dog would urinate on
the bird that lived within. Things were obviously out of control
in this household. The owner had even given up sitting on the
furniture because the dog would come over and leg-lift on *her*. I
guess covering her own legs with plastic or tin foil was where
this owner finally drew the line.

Leg lifting often begins when one or two "shots" go
undisciplined and pheremones are not cleaned up properly. The
first course of action should be to remove as many of the dog's
urination posts as possible. Simply take up wastebaskets or
whatever that can be used as posts. Secondly, the leg-lifter
needs to be confined or, better yet, crated. Some leg-lifters,
however, if crated in open-air crates will simply shoot their

urine out of the sides of the crate, keeping their own area clean and still being able to indulge in their favorite pastime. It might be necessary to get a plastic crate (the kind the airlines use) so that if the leg-lifter lifts his leg, he will urinate on his own premises, which might discourage him from the habit.

*If* you have carefully read the chapter on disciplining after the fact and have determined that your dog is a suitable candidate for such action, you may find that it is harder to find "evidence" of urination when the offender is a leg-lifter, because the urination dries up more quickly—you are left with a nasty stain and no moist evidence.

You may be unintentionally training your dog that leg lifting is okay if you let the dog over-urinate outside. The dog that is allowed to lift its leg on *every* fire hydrant, *every* street sign, *every* lamp post, and is then heartily praised by its owner might take that freedom and praise as a sign to urinate in the house also. If the owner doesn't discipline the dog effectively, or does nothing at all to stop the leg lifting in the house, the dog could be wondering why it isn't getting praised and even try harder (urinate more) to elicit praise. My advice would be to eliminate the constant stops on the street and give the dog only three or four chances to lift his leg. Remember, male dogs always save a little urine instinctively for marking purposes—this is a holdover trait from their wolf days—and so letting the dog urinate until it is "empty" might be a fruitless exercise. Many dogs will simply parcel out their urine drop by drop, hydrant by hydrant.

It is important to realize that constant leg lifting has other meanings to the dog. Ritual leg lifting is a way of marking off territory, and if the dog is a fighter of other dogs, there will often be more leg lifting as the dog renews his claim to the neighborhood turf day by day and even hour by hour. So if the dog has a problem with interspecies fighting, this might have to be solved before leg lifting in the house will get any better. Such dogs will need professional help to quell their aggressive impulses toward other dogs, probably via sessions with a private trainer, and will also need to be enrolled in an obedience class to further expose them to other dogs.

Cut back the water supply of the compulsive leg-lifter

drastically until the problem clears up. Unless your veterinarian directs otherwise, offer only a small amount of water four times a day. A good guide is to offer ¼ cup each time to a very small dog, ½ cup each watering to a medium size dog and 1 cup each time to a large dog. If you have to leave home for over four hours, leave that same amount (no more, and *measure*) in the water bowl. Letting a leg lifter tank up on water all day long will just compound the problem.

Progestin therapy can sometimes be of help to dogs with this problem. Progestins are synthetic compounds related to progesterone. When administered under veterinary supervision, by a veterinarian familiar with proper dosage for behavioral problems, progestins have proven to be of help in cases of urine marking in the house when the behavior is not solely a reflection of inadequate house training. Veterinarians who prescribe Ovaban or other hormonal drugs should, in my opinion, prescribe a competent trainer at the same time. If the client simply gives the drug and does not correct underlying environmental and behavioral reasons for the leg lifting, the problem will probably not get any better, and may get worse. I have found that it is best to go with a very conservative regimen, gradually decreasing the dosage over a 21- to 24-day period. I've found that the dosage prescribed by Schering (the pharmaceutical firm that manufactures Ovaban) for behavioral problems works quite well if the client is also receiving proper advice from a trainer or behaviorist. You might ask your veterinarian about hormonal therapy for your leg-lifter. If one practitioner is not familiar with the use of hormones for behavioral therapy, you might seek out a second opinion.

Finally, if your veterinarian suggests hormone treatment and/or neutering your pet to help with this problem, my advice would be to follow instructions to the letter. Neutering is often indicated and can greatly aid your chances of curing the chronic leg-lifter.

# 14

# Lapses

---

$\mathbf{I}$ ONCE HAD A CLIENT who was a behaviorist—specializing in the human species—who had a ten-year-old Afghan Hound who was seemingly housebroken and had reverted to urinating on every pillar and post in the house. "It's as if he has had lapses in his synapses," he said, referring to the region of contact between neurons across which nerve impulses are transmitted—a process which is essential to thinking things out. "You're right—perhaps," I said and urged him to get a full veterinary checkup for his dog.

Lapses do occur, and in my experience 50 percent of the time there is a medical reason. If you have an older dog who is suddenly leaving "presents" all around the house, my suggestion would be to have an immediate medical checkup. Various problems could be involved, including hormonal difficulties, loss of control due to old age, cysts, tumors, a response to other medications or a response to additives put into the dog's food—especially Vitamin B or Vitamin C.

These vitamins are water soluble and can increase the dog's propensity to urinate. Some dogs will double the number of times they urinate with doses of B or C vitamins circulating in their systems. Puppies have an especially difficult time controlling their bladders if ingesting water-soluble vitamins. Many breeders, especially those who specialize in the larger breeds, are routinely suggesting that their clients use Vitamin C for control of hip dysplasia (although there is no concrete evidence to show that Vitamin C lessens this malady) and other ailments. But they overlook the effect of the vitamin on the housetraining process. It would be better in many instances to complete the housetraining task and then advise addition of these vitamins, if a need is truly indicated.

Older dogs who become "unhousebroken" should be given a complete medical checkup by a veterinarian experienced with geriatric patients. Remember, "old" in many breeds might mean six years of age! Time passes in dog ownership and your friend might indeed be older than you think and even "entitled" to some medical difficulties that might cause lapses. The dog's synapses might be in perfect working order and, chances are, he's as upset about the mistake as you are. Don't discipline this dog—get a diagnosis.

Pregnant bitches often have accidents right and left especially as the whelping date nears. The pressure of puppies and uterine fluids on the bladder is just too much for many bitches and despite their best efforts to maintain control, mistakes happen. While a disgusted scowl is not out of order, it is unfair to discipline the bitch—Lord knows she's got enough on her mind and a big job to do. Cleaning up an accident caused by an overpacked house of potential champion pups is a small price for any breeder to pay. The problem will soon be over after the whelping takes place.

Sometimes, though, a dog isn't old, ill or pregnant and has simply lapsed into lapses. Chances are that the problem is behavioral. If you've carefully ruled out any of the other excuses, and if it is a behavioral problem, chances are that something's wrong with your relationship with your dog. Sorting out behavioral excuses for lapses can be time consuming for any trainer—yet owners desperately want some explanation to why Chuckles now soils the carpet when he never did before.

When I go troubleshooting for causes in such cases I usually trace the dog's history back to point zero—when the owner first procured the dog. And I usually find that the dog was inadequately housetrained or never really housetrained to begin with. The "lapse" is really a flare-up of a dormant condition.

The solution is to crate or confine the dog, umbilical cord it during dinner and during the day, provide as much access to the desired area as possible, feed a high-quality food and offer water *periodically* during the day.

When I said medical reasons were often instrumental in housesoiling lapses I meant it—and don't look only at the present state of the dog's health. Curiously, I've had many cases when an owner of an older dog will report lapses in housetraining in an older dog *after* the dog has had a urinary tract infection or a bout of serious diarrhea. What's going on here?

Drs. Benjamin and Lynette Hart report on such a case in their excellent book *Canine and Feline Behavioral Therapy* (Lea and Febiger, 1985). Preston, a five-year-old Collie, lost sphincter control while battling diarrhea and continued to soil in one distinct spot in the kitchen even after his stool firmed up. "The owner would frequently have to contend with a pile of feces on the kitchen floor," the Harts reported, and "the situation was not improved by warnings, threats or punishment." The tip-off that the problem could be solved was that Preston dumped only on one specific tile of the kitchen floor! In a sense, Preston *was* toilet trained—to eliminate on that one spot. You couldn't ask for more precision—and more frustration. Drs. Hart advised a thorough cleaning of the kitchen, and covering the spot with Preston's sleeping rug—since most dogs do not like to eliminate where they sleep. To prevent Preston from simply selecting another tile for a toilet, the dog was restrained by tethering for a short time until the cycle was broken. In this case we have a mix of medical and behavioral causes for a lapse.

## PURE LAPSES

A "pure lapse" is a break in an already secure housetraining system that has no traceable medical cause, and sometimes no traceable behavioral cause. The first point to remember is that every dog has its day and that day might be a dump-day. These things happen. If the problem occurs once a year and lasts for one day, I really wouldn't worry about it—welcome to dog ownership! Very often a medically and behaviorally sound dog will have an accident when a beloved member of the household exits on a permanent or semipermanent level. If Johnny, who was Rascal's best friend, suddenly goes off to boarding school, Rascal can get a case of anxiety diarrhea and have an accident. Preparations for a vacation bring on a lapse in some dogs. Others lose their housetraining habits at boarding kennels, especially if the kennel is not fastidiously clean. I hasten to add, however, that this is no reason not to board your dog. Simply take care to find a good boarding kennel, preferably one approved by the ABKA (American Boarding Kennels Association) and run by a CKO (Certified Kennel Operator).

## DRIBBLING

Dribbling isn't really a lapse, although its onset can cause an owner to label it as such. It is a common problem in older dogs for whom advancing years have brought with them an inability to hold urine. This dog needs to be walked more frequently— not only to urinate, but to keep his muscle tone in tip-top shape. If the dog's control really suffers a setback, you might have to confine your oldster to one room and cover part of that room with newspaper. It is totally unfair to discipline the dog for behavior now out of its control. Keep your hellos and goodbyes even-keeled and nonanxious, as overemotional greetings or departures can cause the older dog to dribble. Some owners decide to attach a simple absorbent shield to the pet's underside. In fact, it is quite simple to adapt products made for this purpose in older humans to your dog's body.

If you have a puppy or young dog, such measures might seem laughable to you. "Why not just put the dog down?" you might reason. "Isn't it time?" All I can say is that as *your* dog gets older you will not be so quick to prescribe euthanization. As long as the dribbling is not affecting the overall quality of the older dog's life, and assuming it is not coupled with other geriatric problems, I don't consider dribbling a valid excuse for euthanization. As one owner put it to me, "Sam dribbles and his legs are so bad that some days I take him for a walk in my son's wagon, but I really don't mind. I confine him more, and when he's loose, yes, I have to practically follow him with paper towels in hand. But it's a small price to pay for all he's given me and the family. His other problems are not pronounced as yet, and he truly looks sorrowful when he sees me dab up his dribbles. When the day comes when it's not just dribbling, but other health problems, I'll have to make a decision, unless Sam does that himself. And if I have to make the decision, somehow I know he'll tell me with his eyes that it's OK, and that he understands."

# 15

# Pick Up or
# Pay Up

---

**Y**OU MIGHT FEEL a sense of accomplishment once your dog cleans up his act in the house—but you really should clean up after him when he deposits his waste matter where the world has to sidestep it. Cleaning up after your dog, if not the law of the land, is the law in many cities, including New York, Rochester and Buffalo. And such legislation is bound to spread to many other cities.

When the Canine Waste Law was inaugurated by Mayor Koch in New York City in the late 1970s, many people scoffed at the law. Who would obey such a law in a city that is littered with litter-bugs? The first signs that went up were sweet and implored the dog owner to clean up, adding a polite "please." At that point compliance with the law was reasonable, but many New Yorkers still found themselves hesitant to step between parked cars, and on some sidewalks they had to sidestep so many fecal deposits that a simple walk became the equivalent of mastering an obstacle course—trouble was, the "obstacles" were moved each day.

The first signs were sweet. Some even read "Please." Nobody obeyed the law. Note the subtle irony of graffiti over "Keep New York Clean."

Then the city got tough. A fine was levied for abusers of the law and the law was enforced. Compliance soared and is near perfect in many areas of the city today.

The city then got tough. A fine was levied for abusers of the law and—lo and behold—compliance mushroomed. Even today, no one can quite figure it out. Was it the $100 fine? Was it the pride of the dog-owning legions? I think the second. But I will hasten to add that compliance has brought with it definite advantages to that group, and a muting of the criticisms of the non-dog-owning public and even the dog haters (Yes, Mildred, they do exist).

Nowadays, there is peer pressure in New York to clean up after one's pet. I've heard people scream at cheaters, "You creep! What were you—born in a barn?" and even ruder epithets. I've even seen owners clean up after other owners' dogs!

"Yes, everyone laughed at the law when it was first legislated," one long-time New York dog owner told me. I asked her why she thought the law caught on. "Well, you know New Yorkers don't like laws, period," she reflected. "But for dog owners this one came at just the right time. It's something they would have done at a dog show or on someone else's property and they just had to be brought to see the city streets as someone else's property—which they are, you know, they belong to all of us. I remember when the signs said just 'Curb your dog'—so many didn't. It took a law to get us to do what we've always known we should do anyway—and isn't that the perfect use of the law?"

Compliance in New York is far from perfect, but it runs close to 80 percent and that's an inspiration for other cities. My advice to lawmakers in other large cities is to *enact and enforce a strict leash law and clean-up law*. A mysterious phenomenon will occur within five years in any city that does so. The phenomenon will be greater acceptance of dogs by the non-dog-owning public—curious, but true. Who knows what is operable here? Perverse satisfaction on the part of non-dog owners on seeing dog owners perform an unpleasant task? Admiration from city cleanliness cultists? Or perhaps sheer relief from dog owners and the dogless alike for not having to scan the sidewalks so scrupulously?

Whatever the rationale, I would urge you to enact laws in your community—there are definite paybacks. Everyone becomes more tolerant of dogs when there is no need to hurdle their heaps. Dog owners are more likely to observe abnormalities in stools if they have to be retrieved and that means less parasites and worms for all dogs because dogs who are carriers are spotted and treated more quickly.

The myth that dogs are dirty influences much public thinking and decision making. In fact, the Center for Disease Control estimates that from 10 to 30 percent of public playgrounds and parks are contaminated with *Toxocara canis* eggs, the eggs of the common dog roundworm found in infected dogs. So the reasons for cleaning up your dog's act are not strictly aesthetic but also have to do with public health concerns.

Dog owners should remember that dogs have been banned in the capital of Iceland, Peking and on Roosevelt Island in New York City and other areas. I can't help but think that poor pick-up practices and shoddy obedience training have had much to do with such bans. There is a social aspect to keeping a dog and this responsibility extends to cleaning up after your dog.

There has been a barrage of contraptions designed to ease this supposedly terrible task for dog owners. Some are so cumbersome and awkward to handle that they make it difficult for the dog owner to walk the dog while brandishing an oversize pooper-scooper or other such gadget. In the early days of canine waste legislation, such implements were commonly seen in New York City. But since the law has become second-nature, and compliance has risen to all-time highs, most New Yorkers have opted for more serviceable methods of retrieving their dogs' wastes.

While Park Avenue matrons previously attempted to scoop their canine's leftovers into a properly distanced shovel, utilizing a prong that recessed the unpleasantness a full four feet, they now stoop promptly with an inverted plastic bag, capture the refuse and toss it in the nearest waste can. Some New Yorkers are still trying to shove flattened-out newspapers under their defecating pooches, but the majority have invested in reams of plastic bags and have literally "stooped to conquer" the waste problem in New York.

The technique is really very simple. Slip the bag over your

Make it easy on yourself as well as other people. Keep your dog on heel until you get to the appropriate area for elimination. Then, feed the leash out as shown and let the dog sniff. After defecation, put your dog back on the curb and give the sit-stay command and hand signal. Stoop and scoop.

hand, and with your hand thus shielded, pick up after your dog. Then, with your other hand, turn the bag inside out. You'll be able to turn the bag inside out with only one hand within a few tries. Put your dog on a sit-stay *before* you stoop to scrape. If your dog doesn't know a sit-stay, teach it pronto. You will have to clean up at least three times a day and the payoff from a few lessons will be tremendous.

With this method, your hand need never touch the feces. The method is sanitary and safe. You should carry some "twisties" to seal the top of the bag. Think of the maintenance engineer who will have to load that wastebasket onto the garbage truck! The *Cornell Animal Health Newsletter* further advises that you first practice this technique on an orange or a clump of potting soil.

A final tip: foods that are meat-meal based and contain a fiber substance like bran, corn cobs or beet pulp usually result in a firmer, more pick-upable stool, besides being preferable for many other reasons. Soy products or generic dog foods will usually result in floppy stools that need to be scraped up, not picked up. The choice is yours.

If you find all of this gross, in my opinion you've got some reevaluating to do concerning your role as a dog owner. If you are the type who prefers to hide your dog's stool or, worse yet, just lets Rover out to roam and eliminate wherever he desires, you should also realize that you are making it more difficult for other dog owners and for dogs in general. Of course, you probably don't care. That's even worse. It's for people like yourself that Mayor Koch levied the $100 fine. I can only say that if you visit New York and I observe you cheating, I'll make a citizen's arrest.

# 16

# For Trainers

TRAINERS, BEHAVIORISTS and dog-owner counselors are usually well versed in housetraining techniques. While the exact methods might vary from trainer to trainer, as long as the method makes sense, works and is not inhumane, there is little sense debating small flourishes or touches in a given methodology. The important and essential task is the *presentation* of the method to clients. This is where a great many trainers run into difficulties in helping clients with behavior problems with their dogs. Even if the information the trainer wants to give the client is sterling stuff, absolutely reasoned and sound, it will be to no avail if the client can't understand it and grasp it.

In *The Evans Guide for Counseling Dog Owners* (Howell Book House, 1985) I mapped out five different types of dog owners, using a typology borrowed from the family therapist, Virginia Satir. She says that there are five basic stances we take toward each other when communicating. They are: placating, blaming, computing, distracting and leveling. I surmised that dog owners also use these methods of communication in their attempts to get through to their dogs. Since housetraining is often the first real challenge that the owner faces with a dog, it is usually the arena where we can observe the extremes of placating, blaming, computing or distracting.

A tidbit after the dog eliminates? It's not necessary and can lead to canine confusion.

Satir says that these are near universal patterns of communication people use with each other and, may I add, with their dogs:

1. *Placate* so that the other person or the dog doesn't get mad, or in an attempt to get obedience or cooperation.
2. *Blame* so the other person or dog will regard you as strong.
3. *Compute* with the resultant message that you consider the possibility of bad behavior harmless.
4. *Distract* so that you just ignore the behavior as though it were not there.

If we translate these stances to the problem at hand (or under foot, excuse the pun), we can readily see that a distractor personality needs to be educated concerning housetraining in quite a different way than a blamer. For instance, while physical punishment *may* sometimes be in order to correct a chronic housesoiling problem, the physicality must not be overly harsh or inhumane. A blamer personality might be best advised *not* to use physical punishment as he or she will easily go overboard and over-punish, when just the tone of the blamer's voice will be quite enough to convince the dog to clean up its act.

In my work, I've found that the majority of housetraining problems stem from the relationship between a *placating* or *distracting* owner and their dogs. Blamers often terrorize their dogs into cleanliness. Computers are so correct, on time and precise that the dog hardly has a chance to have an accident, let alone be corrected for one. While I usually find computer personalities quite difficult to deal with, this is one area where I can commend them. I rarely get a call from a client experiencing housetraining difficulties and have the client turn out to be a computer.

Placaters are the worst at housetraining since they think they can bribe the dog into cooperation by over-praising it or giving it food when it "performs" in the right place. Placaters are greatly enamored of food as a training tool and usually have a full arsenal of tidbits and treats on hand to stuff down Tippy's throat as soon as elimination occurs. Almost invariably, they will fail to praise the dog *as it eliminates* (placaters are usually spellbound by the process or in the act of giving thanks to God) and will instead call the dog to them *after* elimination is finished and give it a treat. Of course the dog is simply taking the treat for coming when called—not for eliminating. At any rate, food in conjunction with training is simply a dead end, if not today, then tomorrow because it is not historically valid. The bitch never promised to nurse or refused to nurse her puppies if they refrained from defecating on or near her. As Carol Benjamin says succinctly in *Mother Knows Best*, to the bitch, "Food is food and education is education."

Placaters, then, have to be eased out of the food trap and also have to be cautioned about faulty *paralanguage*. If the dog has been whined at in littermate language, it might have been "taught" by the placating owner that truly, there is something wrong with eliminating and especially in the proper place. Many texts instruct owners to stay with the puppy until it eliminates, but for placaters this advice can backfire. As they hover anxiously over the puppy, sniveling and whining at it to "hurrrrie upp, hurriee upp" the pup gets a wonderful lesson in paralanguage: distress and confusion. It would be better if the owner was *not* there. But unless you know how to decode owner characteristics, you will not be able to structure a program for that individual that will contain subtle nuances in technique depending on the personality involved. I would refer you back to *The Evans Guide for Counseling Dog Owners*, with my full support and sympathy as a fellow trainer.

Distractors are perhaps the worst housetrainers as they will tend to simply ignore the problem, hoping that it will go away. I once had a classic distractor who lived in a Park Avenue penthouse of opulent design. She was an heiress of some note and the decor of the apartment was stunning. But as I waited in the foyer for my client to appear, I detected the distinct and eventually overpowering smell of urine. A heavy-set maid, who had immediately impressed me with her savvy and forthrightness when she admitted me to the home, came back into the room, saw my nostrils twitching and said, simply, "I've done everything I can. I can't clean any more!" I knew I was in for an interesting session.

108

Finally my client arrived. She swooped into the room with her Yorkshire Terriers perched on either arm, like parrots. I met Ricky and Ronnie and we proceeded to the den, where the carpet was stained bright yellow.

At first I mistook the spots as parts of the carpet pattern but it quickly became apparent that the carpet was essentially a urination pad. The smell here was even worse than in the foyer. My client began to explain in great detail what great chaps Ricky and Ronnie were, except for one small problem. Expecting, finally, my client to reveal their housetraining disorder I leaned forward, notebook in hand. The problem? "I don't think they love me enough," my client said with an absolutely straight face.

Somewhat flabbergasted (besides needing some air), I asked her what she meant. "Sometimes they ignore me," she explained, "and play with each other." Part of their "ignoring" the client also included urinating in wrong places, but the client didn't present that as the major problem. Nevertheless, knowing that it was, indeed, the *main* difficulty, I plunged on asking questions about walks, feedings and schedules. About this time the maid wandered into the room and continued with her work.

As I queried the owner, the maid positioned herself directly behind her employer, pretending to polish the buffet. When I asked, "How often do you take the dogs out to eliminate," the client answered "Four times a day," but the maid silently mouthed the words "No way!" When I asked how many times the dogs ate each day, the client answered, "Twice," and the maid held up five fingers and made direct eye contact with me.

Catching on to the game, and knowing that I had to get information where I could find it, I continued my line of questioning, prescribed a program based on the maid's answers, ignored almost all of the input from my client and thanked the maid profusely when she ushered me out. "Happy to oblige," she said. "I just want those beasts housebroken before I throttle them!" I called a week later, and the maid had, indeed, house-trained the dogs. The client was busy looking at carpet samples for redecorating and congratulating herself and me on getting her dogs housetrained.

If you have a distractor client, you might not be as lucky as I was to also have a cooperative maid. Simply give the distractor the bare bones of a housetraining program and, most importantly, *write it all out for them.* Distractors cannot grasp more than seven points at any one time so don't overload the circuits. In extreme cases, it might be best to urge the client to send the dog away for housetraining, even though the process should be conducted in the environment in which the dog lives.

If you are a class instructor, don't try to dish out folk remedies to someone experiencing a chronic housetraining problem. Refer that person to a trainer who will come to the home and map out a program in detail, or go yourself. Sometimes clients will enroll in obedience class because of a housetraining problem, thinking that teaching heel, sit, stay, come and down will make the problem "go away." While the owner might become more Alpha and the dog might become more trained, the underlying problem will not be addressed.

Whether you work in class or privately, make sure you *take time* to discuss housetraining matters with your clients and indicate your availability to go over material again in case it is not clear or doesn't seem to apply to an individual case. There is nothing more absurd than a dog who knows the basic exercises and is still not housetrained. A rough equivalent would be an adult with a BA or BS who is not toilet trained. At the first indication of a housetraining problem, corral that client and take him or her aside for a consultation. Often the client just wants to hear from an expert source that certain boundaries are necessary and that the problem will not just "go away" in time. Such clients need you to set down the boundaries and ground rules verbally, even if they would be the same rules they themselves would like to implement. A simple statement like, "You must not tolerate accidents in the house any longer" goes a long way and spurs the client to get the housetraining task over, once and for all.

# 17

# Special Advice for Breeders, Pet Store Operators and Animal Shelter Personnel

ALTHOUGH IT HAS NOT BEEN discussed much in print, those professionals who raise puppies, whether by avocation or default, can often make the difference between whether a puppy or older dog gets housetrained, simply by the way we structure or fail to structure our rearing environments. In traveling coast to coast in the United States and Canada, I'm often amazed that even seasoned professionals do not seem to realize that the bitch would like to start the housetraining task once solid food is introduced (see Chapter 2, "In the Beginning: The Bitch"). Some breeders even thwart her efforts by not providing enough space for the bitch to send her

Is this puppy, waiting in a pet store for an owner to take him home, getting off to a good or bad start in the housetraining process?

puppies to in order to take care of their elimination needs. Further, some breeders, pet store operators and animal shelter personnel compound these structural failings by educational mistakes—they simply fail to give their clients sufficient advice concerning housetraining, and, in some cases, just lie to the client in order to make a sale.

For instance, it is common for pet store operators to claim that a puppy or older dog is "paper trained" when in fact the dog has never lived in a house and has never urinated or defecated on any surface *other* than newspaper since it was born! That fact *does not* mean that a puppy is "paper trained" and can be turned loose in a household and trusted to find the paper when it is hidden around three or four difficult turns.

What the pet store operator *should* say is, simply, that the puppy has been urinating and defecating on paper and is used to eliminating on that surface, but the pup should be kept confined so that the paper is readily available. Unfortunately, as long as paper training is seen as a "service" that the pet store has performed for the owner, and as long as owners view a puppy as a little machine that can be purchased "trained" it will be difficult to halt this kind of deception.

On the other hand, false promises are not always malicious or an attempt to con the owner. Often good-hearted shelter personnel will say that a given dog is housetrained simply because they have no reason to believe otherwise. Dr. Myrna Milani, DVM, put it well in *The Weekend Dog:*

> Many times busy people get adult dogs from humane societies with the idea that these animals will be housebroken. Actually, quite often the opposite is true. Many animals wind up in such places because they *aren't* housebroken. Unfortunately, the original owners' feelings of guilt and inadequacy prevented them from revealing the problem to the personnel of the animal shelter. If the shelter places such a dog in a small kennel, no problem will be detected until the new owners find the puddles and piles in their homes.

I'd only add that it is precisely then that the new owners return the same dog to the shelter, and the cycle starts again, or the dog is euthanized. A solution would be to give each shelter animal ten to fifteen minutes of free-roaming time each day and monitor who has accidents. Ideally, the time period would be longer, so that the dog could even have the chance to go to a door and whine to be let out, or otherwise indicate that it has to eliminate. Indeed, I've been in some shelters where selected free-roaming periods within the confines of the shelter are standard practice. This gives shelter personnel a chance to observe behavior that would never manifest itself when the dog is in a cage. Remember, even if the dog *was* truly housetrained in its former home, it needs to be retrained to the new owner's schedule and structure.

The point in all this is that breeders, pet store operators and shelter personnel *must* educate themselves in housetraining procedures and take a careful look at the structures and schedules they use to whelp and rear dogs until placement age. Housetraining is *not* a task that you assign to the owner with expressions of sympathy or false hopes. In a great many ways, the housetraining process begins with you and is simply *continued* by the owner.

## BREEDERS

To aid your clients in housetraining, and to spare yourself endless hours on the phone answering questions about it, structure your whelping and rearing environments to maximize the puppy's natural desire to keep its area clean, and allow the bitch to act like the Alpha she is and begin the housetraining process. During the first three weeks of life, keep the whelping box very clean. Check. Don't depend on the bitch to take care of all refuse. If you use shredded paper, shred it *thin* so that defecation that is not immediately consumed by the mother will drop through and not stick to the shredded paper. Clean the whelping box *twice* a day—in the morning and before retiring. Take all of the paper out and put fresh paper (or whatever bedding you use) in the box, after swabbing out the whelping box. One time a day is not enough. Remember, puppies can smell, and the smell of urine and defecation early in life doesn't help the housetraining process later on.

Puppies should be born within the *interior* of the household

114

so that the pups see and hear the sights and sounds of a normal household. I hope that you are a responsible breeder and are raising *real* puppies that will live with *real* people in *real* homes and that you are not a backyard breeder raising junk puppies destined to live in backyards. If you fall into the latter group, you probably won't be reading this book, and you probably don't even care about housetraining since the dog lives outdoors. But that's truly a dog's life. Don't use garages or basements for whelping litters. These areas inevitably lead to isolation for the pups, and a lack of socialization.

If you provide an area within the interior of the home you are going to be there to monitor the pup's progress and to make sure that the whelping area is clean. You just can't do this if the puppies are shunted off to a far-away place and only visited once or twice a day.

Don't leave the pups in the whelping box longer than 3 to 3½ weeks, regardless of breed and regardless of litter size. It might be convenient for *you* to leave them in such a confined area to facilitate clean up, and the bitch might be quite cooperative about consuming stools even into the fourth week and after solid food has been introduced, but *do* get the pups out into a larger area. Preferably this area would be about 6 × 8 feet or 9 × 12 feet, with just one half of the room covered with papers (at least three thick and laid flat), with shredded paper on top of those papers. Start even at this age to divide the three major functions of elimination, eating and drinking and sleeping. Elimination, of course, occurs in the papered area, eating and drinking can take place in another corner (as far from the paper as possible) and sleeping materials (not newspaper or any bedding resembling the elimination surface) can be in a third area.

It is a rare puppy who will make mistakes if given this amount of space. Almost all will make it to the paper. If you have pups who are not getting the idea, leave the paper down for just one day without cleaning (perhaps you can shred some more paper over stools that have already been deposited) so that the slower puppies will mimic the others and have some stools to "guide" them.

If you color code your pups with ric-rac or other colored collars you might be able to tell which pup consistently has accidents off the paper. Obviously, you want to place this puppy with experienced people who will be able to provide access to an appropriate area for elimination quite frequently during the day. In the same way, the more responsible pups can be placed in homes in which they might have to "hold it" a little longer. Of course, housetraining aptitude is not the only aspect an intelligent breeder looks at when trying to match puppies with the right people but it is one aspect that, in my experience, is often discounted or ignored. Remember, when the new owner comes for the pup, he or she is full of love and hope for a great relationship. It will be the housetraining process that will introduce the first sour notes in the new friendship. Do a little evaluation by observing the litter, taking some notes and using the information you glean in your placement process.

If the pups outgrow this area, which they will by the time they are eight weeks of age (possibly before that if the litter is large), and you must move the pups to a larger space, try to duplicate the set-up in the house as closely as you can. Often an indoor area connected to an outdoor area by a swing door can be very valuable. You can put the bitch into the area to teach the puppies how to use the door. They will chase her in and out of the indoor and outdoor areas and learn to push the door open. It's best to make the indoor area smaller than the outdoor space, so that the pups will want to use that area as their eating/sleeping/denning area and will go out the door to use the outside area as an elimination site. If you have a dog run, often with a little creativity and carpentry you can make some adjustments to provide this kind of a set-up. You will have performed a service to your clients because you will be placing puppies who already *want* to eliminate outside and keep their indoor area clean. If the new owner can install a dog door, so much the better. Breeders who structure their environments along these lines often report that their clients report housetraining success in two or three *days!*

Contrast the responsible breeder who makes an effort to provide a proper environment with the irresponsible breeder.

This breeder stations the whelping box out in the garage ("We don't have enough room in the house and the kids go out and play with them for ten minutes each day") and works 9 to 5 every weekday. First, if you don't have an area within the interior of your household to whelp your pups, in my opinion, you don't belong in breeding. Secondly, I fail to see how you can keep the puppy area clean if you are gone all day long, not to mention socialize the puppies. During the day, especially after the third week when solid food is introduced and the stools are larger, the puppies will perform the Mexican Hat Dance on them all day long as they play and cavort with each other. You will come home to a whelping box full of mashed down stools and urine. The puppies will learn to live in their own filth. Future owners will have more difficulty housetraining these pups. You must be there to clean.

Finally, as a breeder you owe it to your clients to spend time educating them about how to handle housetraining starting with the moment they get their pup home. *Ask* whether they intend to paper train or outdoor train, when they will be home to give the pup access to the desired site, what they intend to feed, when water will be offered and how much. As a former breeder for over a decade and now in my work as a private trainer in the home I find that many breeders fail to give housetraining information or to inquire about the nuts and bolts of the owner's environment. When I was a breeder at the monastery (I know that sounds contradictory!) I know I had to force myself to *envision the owner's environment* in order to give proper advice on how to conduct housetraining in each individual case. Inquire about the layout of the home, about how many turns the pup will have to make to get to the proper area for elimination, about *how* confined the pup will be and about past dogs and their housetraining success (or lack of it). Obviously, if a client comes to you and indicates, even in passing, that they had a dog and had difficulty housetraining it, don't assume that they got stuck with a clinker pup and were doing everything right—chances are, they blew it. Map out your housetraining regimen, verbally *and* on paper. In addition, *act it out* for your clients by demonstrating with the puppy how to correct mistakes and how to praise when the pup performs in the right place. Most of all, unless the client is an experienced dog person, please don't assume that they know how to housetrain a dog. Remember, the state of dog care and training is where child care and training was 100 years ago—and housetraining is the area most glutted with myth and folklore. Go over the information even if you think you're boring them and be sure to provide it in written form (via a book or your own handout) so that they can refer to it at home. Finally, indicate that there *will* be some accidents and that accidents are actually *desirable* because they give the owner an opportunity to educate the dog. Tell your clients to call you if they have difficulties, but be sure you have envisioned their environment while you have time with them in person, because it is much harder to do it over the phone.

## PET STORE OPERATORS

Some pet stores are kept scrupulously clean and sanitized, others are not. Some pet stores procure puppies from reputable breeders who began the housetraining process correctly, others get their stock from Midwest puppy mills where sanitation is not a priority.

Ideally, every potential pet owner would go to a caring breeder and have a puppy carefully matched to them by an intelligent, people-wise and puppy-wise breeder, who would then offer to be of help and counsel for the life of the dog. This happens sometimes, but often owners procure a pup from a bad breeder or a pet store that just doesn't care. There is no attempt made to match the right pup with the right person, and buyers may have no outlet except a disgruntled or inexperienced employee who hangs up on them when they call to ask for a shred of advice. I really have nothing against pet stores *per se*, and I am enough of a realist to know that they are not going to go out of business and that a great many people "impulse buy" from such outlets. I have also trained puppies from pet stores that were of extraordinary intelligence and poise—and frequently good specimens of their given breeds. But, to be honest, in the area of housetraining, my records over the last fifteen years show a plethora of housetraining problems from pet store puppies. Why is this so?

Part of the problem stems from the original environment in which the puppies were born. Pet store puppies are often, but not always, conceived on "puppy farms" in a Midwestern state (Kansas and Nebraska come to mind immediately) that has very lenient regulations concerning the raising of puppies. Such establishments are commonly called "puppy mills." Puppies that get a start in puppy mills are often shunted from pen to pen, and are sometimes weaned prior to the fourth week, so that the mother doesn't have a chance to act as an Alpha and establish basic rules of cleanliness. As early as the fourth or fifth week these pups are often crated and in the air on their way to a pet store, so that they will arrive for public display at their cutest age—eight to ten weeks. Their sales potential is then greatly enhanced, but their housetraining potential is greatly diminished in most cases.

During the time they are with their mothers they are clean enough, but the bitch is removed too quickly (often to dry her up milk-wise and get her ready for another litter). Because of this the pups never have the benefit of her guiding hand (paw!) for socialization and housetraining purposes.

After the separation from mom, these puppy mill "children" are often caged in substandard holds, often with flooring that either allows them to mash their stools and urine or allows it to drop through wire to the ground. Depending on the arrangements made, the airline flight to Chicago, Los Angeles or New York pet stores can be harrowing, often involving hours of time with the pups reclining in their own refuse. It's not a good start for a puppy, especially in the area of housetraining.

When the pups arrive at the pet store, they are often kept in cages in a back room and then deposited in window display areas to encourage impulse buyers. Finely shredded paper might be provided, or, in some stores, drainage systems or trays may be installed beneath the display pen, but the pups inevitably defecate, urinate, step on and play in their waste. The buying public sees only cute puppies cavorting and acrobating in seemingly clean shredded paper, but underneath the paper are packed down piles of stools and urine. Even if the pet store operator changes the paper several times a day, if even *one stool* is spread around when pups play, the resulting message to the pups is *not* one of the necessity of keeping their area clean.

It would be better for the pet store operator to provide a double-sectioned pen; one section would hold papers and would be changed frequently and another section would be a play and "display" area. Pet store operators should remember that they are already working against a bad housetraining background for many pups, and it is best to provide some introduction to clean habits before sending the pups home to their new owners. Finally, pet store operators, while not always capable or available to give on-the-spot advice on housetraining matters, should at least provide a good selection of books on the topic and direct their clients to these texts.

## SHELTER PERSONNEL

Anyone who has worked longer than two seconds at an animal shelter knows that one of the chief reasons owners drop off unwanted pets is that they are not housetrained. Shelter personnel tend to be very world-wise and savvy, and they know that when an owner comes in and says, "We have to move," that's English for "He poops" (or piddles or chews or digs or whatever verb is appropriate). Shelter personnel often hear phrases like, "He's not as *clean* as I thought he would be, but I'm sure he would be for someone else," or "He might have a few accidents in his new home but he's really a doll." All these statements mean the dog is not housebroken and the owners who adopt should be so informed. There should be a form that is used within each shelter to decode such problems and animals that cannot be placed and that harbor such problems might simply have to be moved up on the list of animals to be euthanized.

Before the humaniacs starting hooting and hollering let me say that I have paid my dues in shelter work. I have seen the pain that is involved on both the human and canine end (no matter how benign the euthanization method) when a dog must be eliminated. I do not like the procedure nor the phenomenon. I stress again for the benefit of my shelter readers, *I have been there*, euthanizing dogs: the butterfly syringe, the push on the needle cap, the actual flow of the injection fluid, the slight quirk, the strange stillness, the limpness, the collapse, the end.

Because I have been there, I am dedicated to educating the public on the absolute imperative of getting the pup housetrained quickly and effectively, and of providing proper training throughout the dog's life. But I am also a realist, and I know that we have a large surplus of animals waiting for homes. Why place a dog that is known to be a chronic housesoiler? It just doesn't make sense, unless the dog has other appealing qualities *and* a potential owner who is fully aware of the problem and willing to work with it, patiently and consistently. Any other owner will sour on the dog quite quickly and either return it to the shelter or just abuse it.

Shelter personnel should also have on hand a variety of books, leaflets and pamphlets that outline housetraining procedures. Often clients will leave the shelter completely in the dark as to what to do once they get the puppy home, and will subsequently bungle the housetraining process. A simple pamphlet or, better yet, a short consultation *and* a pamphlet at the shelter would have prevented many a returned puppy.

Again, it is not my intention to criticize shelter personnel. Such souls are, in my opinion, saints. They are living on the front line of the humane movement. Nor is it my intention to lampoon pet store operators, although, frankly, I wish all pet stores sold was food and supplies. Further, I do not have it in for breeders—only those backyard breeders who thwart the socialization needs of their pups and their housetraining needs by providing substandard conditions.

My hope (perhaps naive) is that standards throughout the industry and fancy will improve with continued education so that we provide environments in which "cleanliness is next to godliness" and thus our pups can clear the housetraining hurdle in their new homes with ease and grace.

# Closing Note

I HOPE by now you have my methodology for getting your pooch perfect clear in your mind, and have begun to restructure your environment to allow for proper confinement, and re-ordered your thoughts to allow for proper correction. I'm also sure (I am, aren't I?) that you've selected a top quality ration for your pet and that you've established a schedule that is considerate of your dog's needs. In short, I hope you've put into effect the ACCESS plan for success in housetraining your dog. Now, there is one last thing I'd like to ask of you.

I'd like you to be sure to drop any lingering *anger* you might have toward your dog over past mistakes, because the emotion of anger has within it subtleties that your dog will pick up via your body language and paralanguage. If you are intent on blaming your dog for all past, present and future mistakes, housetraining might take longer. Anger alienates your dog from you and deprives you of your true Alpha-role. Far better to just *act angry* when disciplining than to really be filled with rage over a urine or defecation spot.

Here's an example of the inordinate anger that I'm indicating, and that I feel stalls the housetraining process. I once had a client with a rather sweet Yorkshire Terrier who was leaving stool and urine presents all over the house. When the client first called, she asked me if it was true that dogs of this breed "can never be housebroken." She said that's what she had heard.

My reply to her was to be very careful about "facts" she heard from laypersons (for that matter, from some professionals) about dogs who can or can't do this or that. The fact is, Yorkies aren't any more difficult to housetrain than any other breed, but I think some owners *put up* with accidents longer from dogs of this size because the mistakes are easily hidden and when found, easily cleaned. As one client once put it to me, "I put up with it because I can clean up." That's true until putting up and cleaning up become frustrating and then the owner calls a trainer, blaming the dog.

But no matter how carefully I tried to educate this client, both on the phone and during my in-home consultation with her, she continued to maintain the fiction that this particular breed just couldn't be housetrained and that the dog was doing it "all for spite." Naturally, she abrogated the ACCESS program to fit her daily whims, changing confinement quarters constantly, forgetting the schedule, feeding junk foods and over-correcting her dog by chasing the little critter around the house with a spatula or hairbrush. My last communication with her was a frustrated message on my answering machine that delivered an ultimatum: "Mr. Evans, either Sukiyaki is going to die, or I'm going to commit suicide!" She never got Sukiyaki housetrained—and I think her anger, which probably could be ascribed to other frustrations, thwarted her efforts. Don't be angry with your unhousetrained monster, *act angry,* when appropriate.

If you find yourself still bewildered about the ACCESS process, do go back and re-read the chapters that are appropriate. Sometimes it helps to have another person in the household read over the information also, because you might have missed something. Remember, if you have several persons residing with the dog, *all* parties must know the basics of the ACCESS plan, especially the house rules for confinement and the specific methods of correction. In some families, the schedule has to be pow-wowed about to be sure everyone fulfills his or her obligations to walk the dog or provide the dog with access to the desired area for elimination. If one family member consistently slips up, refuses to correct the dog, or shelves the battle plan, the housetraining task will be delayed, if not stymied. Housetraining your dog is, indeed, a *family affair*—your dog *is* a member of the family, isn't he?

I hope that you will spread this information to other dog owners, as well—especially to those who just "expect" their dogs to be housetrained overnight or who are bungling the process badly. Housetraining isn't just something that magically happens. I wish it did, but that's not reality. It's hard work, for a time, and then it's done, if you do it right the first time. That's the nice thing about housetraining: once it's done, it's done. I know that; now you know that. Tell others.

And one last request, a small one, a personal one. Wherever your dog is right now, go give him a hug for me. Go ahead. There's just one exception for which he goes hugless—well, you know what it is, and you know what to do.

# INDEX

# BIBLIOGRAPHY

ALL OWNERS of pure-bred dogs will benefit themselves and their dogs by enriching their knowledge of breeds and of canine care, training, breeding, psychology and other important aspects of dog management. The following list of books covers further reading recommended by judges, veterinarians, breeders, trainers and other authorities. Books may be obtained at the finer book stores and pet shops, or through Howell Book House Inc., publishers, New York.

## BREED BOOKS

| | |
|---|---|
| AFGHAN HOUND, Complete | Miller & Gilbert |
| AIREDALE, New Complete | Edwards |
| AKITA, Complete | Linderman & Funk |
| ALASKAN MALAMUTE, Complete | Riddle & Seeley |
| BASSET HOUND, New Complete | Braun |
| BLOODHOUND, Complete | Brey & Reed |
| BOXER, Complete | Denlinger |
| BRITTANY SPANIEL, Complete | Riddle |
| BULLDOG, New Complete | Hanes |
| BULL TERRIER, New Complete | Eberhard |
| CAIRN TERRIER, New Complete | Marvin |
| CHESAPEAKE BAY RETRIEVER, Complete | Cherry |
| CHIHUAHUA, Complete | Noted Authorities |
| COCKER SPANIEL, New | Kraeuchi |
| COLLIE, New | Official Publication of the Collie Club of America |
| DACHSHUND, The New | Meistrell |
| DALMATIAN, The | Treen |
| DOBERMAN PINSCHER, New | Walker |
| ENGLISH SETTER, New Complete | Tuck, Howell & Graef |
| ENGLISH SPRINGER SPANIEL, New | Goodall & Gasow |
| FOX TERRIER, New | Nedell |
| GERMAN SHEPHERD DOG, New Complete | Bennett |
| GERMAN SHORTHAIRED POINTER, New | Maxwell |
| GOLDEN RETRIEVER, New Complete | Fischer |
| GORDON SETTER, Complete | Look |
| GREAT DANE, New Complete | Noted Authorities |
| GREAT DANE, The—Dogdom's Apollo | Draper |
| GREAT PYRENEES, Complete | Strang & Giffin |
| IRISH SETTER, New Complete | Eldredge & Vanacore |
| IRISH WOLFHOUND, Complete | Starbuck |
| JACK RUSSELL TERRIER, Complete | Plummer |
| KEESHOND, New Complete | Cash |
| LABRADOR RETRIEVER, New Complete | Warwick |
| LHASA APSO, Complete | Herbel |
| MALTESE, Complete | Cutillo |
| MASTIFF, History and Management of the | Baxter & Hoffman |
| MINIATURE SCHNAUZER, New | Kiedrowski |
| NEWFOUNDLAND, New Complete | Chern |
| NORWEGIAN ELKHOUND, New Complete | Wallo |
| OLD ENGLISH SHEEPDOG, Complete | Mandeville |
| PEKINGESE, Quigley Book of | Quigley |
| PEMBROKE WELSH CORGI, Complete | Sargent & Harper |
| POODLE, New | Irick |
| POODLE CLIPPING AND GROOMING BOOK, Complete | Kalstone |
| PORTUGUESE WATER DOG, Complete | Braund & Miller |
| ROTTWEILER, Complete | Freeman |
| SAMOYED, New Complete | Ward |
| SCOTTISH TERRIER, New Complete | Marvin |
| SHETLAND SHEEPDOG, The New | Riddle |
| SHIH TZU, Joy of Owning | Seranne |
| SHIH TZU, The (English) | Dadds |
| SIBERIAN HUSKY, Complete | Demidoff |
| TERRIERS, The Book of All | Marvin |
| WEIMARANER, Guide to the | Burgoin |
| WEST HIGHLAND WHITE TERRIER, Complete | Marvin |
| WHIPPET, Complete | Pegram |
| YORKSHIRE TERRIER, Complete | Gordon & Bennett |

## BREEDING

| | |
|---|---|
| ART OF BREEDING BETTER DOGS, New | Onstott |
| BREEDING YOUR OWN SHOW DOG | Seranne |
| HOW TO BREED DOGS | Whitney |
| HOW PUPPIES ARE BORN | Prine |
| INHERITANCE OF COAT COLOR IN DOGS | Little |

## CARE AND TRAINING

| | |
|---|---|
| BEYOND BASIC DOG TRAINING | Bauman |
| COUNSELING DOG OWNERS, Evans Guide for | Evans |
| DOG OBEDIENCE, Complete Book of | Saunders |
| NOVICE, OPEN AND UTILITY COURSES | Saunders |
| DOG CARE AND TRAINING FOR BOYS AND GIRLS | Saunders |
| DOG NUTRITION, Collins Guide to | Collins |
| DOG TRAINING FOR KIDS | Benjamin |
| DOG TRAINING, Koehler Method of | Koehler |
| DOG TRAINING Made Easy | Tucker |
| GO FIND! Training Your Dog to Track | Davis |
| GROOMING DOGS FOR PROFIT | Gold |
| GUARD DOG TRAINING, Koehler Method of | Koehler |
| MOTHER KNOWS BEST—The Natural Way to Train Your Dog | Benjamin |
| OPEN OBEDIENCE FOR RING, HOME AND FIELD, Koehler Method of | Koehler |
| STONE GUIDE TO DOG GROOMING FOR ALL BREEDS | Stone |
| SUCCESSFUL DOG TRAINING, The Pearsall Guide to | Pearsall |
| TEACHING DOG OBEDIENCE CLASSES—Manual for Instructors | Volhard & Fisher |
| TOY DOGS, Kalstone Guide to Grooming All | Kalstone |
| TRAINING THE RETRIEVER | Kersley |
| TRAINING TRACKING DOGS, Koehler Method of | Koehler |
| TRAINING YOUR DOG—Step by Step Manual | Volhard & Fisher |
| TRAINING YOUR DOG TO WIN OBEDIENCE TITLES | Morsell |
| TRAIN YOUR OWN GUN DOG, How to | Goodall |
| UTILITY DOG TRAINING, Koehler Method of | Koehler |
| VETERINARY HANDBOOK, Dog Owner's Home | Carlson & Giffin |

## GENERAL

| | |
|---|---|
| A DOG'S LIFE | Burton & Allaby |
| AMERICAN KENNEL CLUB 1884-1984—A Source Book | American Kennel Club |
| CANINE TERMINOLOGY | Spira |
| COMPLETE DOG BOOK, The | Official Publication of American Kennel Club |
| DOG IN ACTION, The | Lyon |
| DOG BEHAVIOR, New Knowledge of | Pfaffenberger |
| DOG JUDGE'S HANDBOOK | Tietjen |
| DOG PSYCHOLOGY | Whitney |
| DOGSTEPS, The New | Elliott |
| DOG TRICKS | Haggerty & Benjamin |
| EYES THAT LEAD—Story of Guide Dogs for the Blind | Tucker |
| FRIEND TO FRIEND—Dogs That Help Mankind | Schwartz |
| FROM RICHES TO BITCHES | Shattuck |
| HAPPY DOG/HAPPY OWNER | Siegal |
| IN STITCHES OVER BITCHES | Shattuck |
| JUNIOR SHOWMANSHIP HANDBOOK | Brown & Mason |
| OUR PUPPY'S BABY BOOK (blue or pink) | |
| SUCCESSFUL DOG SHOWING, Forsyth Guide to | Forsyth |
| WHY DOES YOUR DOG DO THAT? | Bergman |
| WILD DOGS in Life and Legend | Riddle |
| WORLD OF SLED DOGS, From Siberia to Sport Racing | Coppinger |